Better to Speak of It:
Fostering Relationships & Results Through Creativity

Arch Street Press
Bryn Mawr

Arch Street Press
Bryn Mawr, PA · USA

First Arch Street Press edition October 2016

ARCH STREET PRESS, ARCH ST. PRESS
and colophon are registered trademarks of Arch Street Press.

For information about special discounts for bulk and nonprofit purchases, please contact Arch Street Press: sales@archstreetpress.org.

Cover painting by Jessica Libor

Library of Congress Cataloging-in-Publication Data is available.

All direct quotes from UK citizens use the British spellings.

ISBN: 978-1-938798-09-2
ISBN: 978-1-938798-11-5 (e-book)

Dedications

Heartfelt thanks to Emanuel Ax, Joyce DiDonato, Paul King, Joel Klein, Dvora Lewis, Glenn Lowry, Lennox Mackenzie, Philip Maneval, Ian Martin, Anthony Marx, Anne-Sophie Mutter, Jessye Norman, Joseph Polisi, Matías Tarnopolsky, Michael Tilson Thomas, Jonathan Vaughan and Allison Vulgamore. Beyond vital contributions to this book through interviews and correspondence, their devotion to education and society on both sides of the stage has had an enduring worldwide impact.

Robert Rimm

With gratitude to my colleagues above, and with all my love and admiration to my children: Sarah, Miriam and David, my most beloved and valuable teachers in life.

Clive Gillinson

Contents

Communication & Media

Looking Inward

Prelude: The Birth of Fulfillment

"As a cellist in the London Symphony Orchestra (LSO), there was one thing about which I was absolutely certain: I would never, ever want to manage an orchestra! I knew that, as a musician, I was living in the creative world, and we musicians viewed management as routine paper pushers. In fact, the best man at my wedding was Michael Kaye, the LSO manager at the time, and I remember asking him, perhaps a little insensitively, why on earth he had ever wanted to do the job. Ironically," Clive Gillinson recalls from his office at Carnegie Hall, where he is its executive and artistic director, "becoming a manager was the first time since being a music student that I started to live my life as an artist; playing in an orchestra had increasingly become like being a highly skilled worker. That is why I think seeking to travel predetermined career paths is so dangerous for young people, as perception and reality are almost always entirely different; little is what you expect it to be, nor should it be! I decided to go into music because I wanted to spend my life as a creative artist, yet I soon discovered that playing in a great orchestra—while wonderful in many ways—can become hugely frustrating. Equally, I had always assumed that being a manager would be routine and boring, and I didn't have the slightest interest in it as a career. Both preconceptions could not have been more wrong."

Throughout almost everyone's life, opportunities arise to explore new paths that are rarely visible at the time:

"Your life can take myriad directions. If your eyes are open, if you're interested, if you're curious, if you're exploring, if you always want to know and understand more, significant opportunities will inevitably arise. Do most of us know where life will ultimately take us? Absolutely not! An apparently small coincidence can become the most important turning point of one's life, although completely invisible at the time. When I left the Royal Academy of Music, I auditioned for London's two leading orchestras at that time: the Philharmonia and the London Symphony Orchestra. I most wanted to join the LSO because to me they represented excitement, passion and risk, but they had no openings in the cello section, so I was delighted to be offered a job in the Philharmonia and accepted. My first three months were extraordinary, playing in Otto Klemperer's historic last Beethoven cycle, whilst sitting next to my mother in the cello section. Then the phone rang; someone had just left the LSO cello section and would I like the job? I leapt at the offer. Had I declined, or had that job not opened up, I would almost certainly never have become a manager. Totally by chance my entire life had changed, and I did not have the slightest idea that this had happened. I knew that the LSO was where I wanted to be, so I didn't hesitate to take the job. However, not only was I never remotely interested in becoming a manager, I would never have become one had the orchestra not hit the rocks! The Philharmonia never faced a financial disaster during or after my cello-playing days, so transferring into management would never have crossed my radar had I stayed there."

Gillinson served on the LSO's board of directors during two periods: one earlier on as finance director and then from 1983, when he was asked to join again because the orchestra had run into serious financial problems, with a massive and growing deficit. The LSO had moved into the newly built Barbican Centre in March 1982, and the manager had adopted an American orchestra-subscription model that bore no relation to the way London's musical life worked. Money was pouring out the door as the orchestra played night after night to half-empty halls—a totally demoralizing experience for the players, not to mention the audiences. Despite the picture growing ever more bleak, the manager refused to adapt, convinced that the public funding bodies would not let the LSO fail and would have to put in more money to save it. Neither the board nor Gillinson shared this belief. He could either have continued to concentrate solely on his job as a cellist or try to play a part in attempting to save the orchestra. By the time he joined the board again, it had already sacked the manager.

Because they had received no viable applications for the job, the board decided—in desperation—to put a player into the office while they looked for a manager:

"They asked two of us to do the job, for one month each, the vice chairman and I, after which they would decide who would continue to hold the fort, if needed. At the end of our 'trials' they had still not found a real manager, and asked me to do the job for a further three months whilst they continued the search. At the end of that time, they still hadn't found anyone and offered me the job. I had no belief that I could do it and no desire to at that point. The only thing that convinced me to at least give it a try was the fact that they thought I was capable of it—I certainly didn't! However, I said to them that after three months there was no way they could know if I was the right person for the job, and no way that I knew if I wanted it. I therefore offered to do the job for a year, with the proviso that they keep my position in the cello section open. If at the end of that time they didn't want me or I didn't want the job, I'd go back to playing in the orchestra. That first year, hauling the orchestra back from the edge of bankruptcy, was horrendous, definitely not helped by the fact that I knew absolutely nothing about management. The one positive aspect was that I knew and understood the players, but that seemed like a minor advantage at the time, compared with the financial disaster we were facing. Luckily there were some terrific people on the management team, and we worked together to develop a strategy to fight our way back. In addition to the massive demands of the job, our twins had also been born around that time, so I nearly forgot what it was like to sleep…. Between work and night feeding, it was as if I was seeing life through a gauze veil caused by sheer exhaustion; nothing was clear anymore. One thing I did learn at that time was the meaning of the phrase 'ignorance is bliss.' Had I known just how hard the job was going to be, I doubt I would ever have taken it on."

Gillinson's competitive nature asserted itself and he refused to give up. He began to feel that maybe he could succeed, and for the first time in his life considered that he might have some capacity for leadership. He felt confident as a cellist, but had reluctantly come to accept that he would not make it as a soloist. Although playing in an orchestra had not been his first aspiration, it was a good living with many great concerts, fascinating tours around the world, exciting film-music scores such as the *Star Wars* series, *Superman, Raiders of the Lost Ark, ET* and many more, and great camaraderie. Also, he had gotten into the orchestra he most admired:

"There was nothing more thrilling than making music with extraordinary conductors such as Leonard Bernstein or Claudio Abbado. However, many of the conductors with whom we worked at that time were good rather than great, and a few were not even good! On one infamous occasion the LSO was engaged to make a Haydn symphony recording with a mediocre, unknown conductor. We were recording the scherzo of the Haydn and it was a mess; the conductor just could not get everyone to play together. In the end the recording company suggested that the conductor go into the recording booth to listen, whilst the orchestra's concertmaster conducted the movement, so the conductor could identify where the problems lay. He listened and said it sounded fine, and recorded it once more himself. The next year, to the delight of the conductor, his recording won a major prize. No one had the heart to tell him that the issued recording was of the performance conducted by the concertmaster, not by the conductor himself! Over time, the inconsistency of standards eroded the job's enjoyment for many of the players, often diminishing the love of music that had led them into the profession in the first place. Idealism, such a central part of life at the Royal Academy of Music and previously in the National Youth Orchestra, became a relative rarity."

Gillinson is acutely aware of the unanticipated circumstances that led him to Carnegie Hall. "If I had mapped a career path for myself, there isn't the slightest chance that I'd be running Carnegie Hall today, or any other day for that matter!" he reflects with a quiet laugh that suggests both wonder and gratitude.

"Yes, I was open to opportunities, but I have absolutely no idea why I was the guy they asked to stand in as manager at the LSO all those years ago; I sometimes wonder if I was the last person out the door! I thought they were mad to ask me, but it was the turning point in my life."

Circumstance

That life began during the Second World War, when Gillinson's mother concertized throughout Palestine and Egypt, often for the British troops. She had been building a top-level career in Europe as a soloist, including performing the Dvořák Cello Concerto with the Czech Philharmonic Orchestra conducted by Rafael Kubelík, a tremendous achievement for a young player. However, her career was cut short by the rise of the Nazis and her departure for Palestine. Gillinson's father was fighting with the British Army in Iraq and went on leave to Palestine, where he attended one of her concerts. He had wanted to visit Palestine because of his own Jewish roots. At the end of her concert, he contrived to travel back with her in a taxi, fell in love and asked to meet with her the next day, whereupon he gave her a beautiful watch engraved RG. When she asked him what RG stood for, he said: "Regina Gillinson. We're going to get married!" Their son was conceived on their wedding night in Palestine, and born in India.

Gillinson's father demonstrated a clear creative bent as a writer and painter. However, not able to satisfy his desire to become an artist himself, he was overwhelmed by his wife's beauty and artistry; she represented everything that he had dreamed of for his own life. At the end of the war, the couple left for India because his parents were living there and, like most of the young men who joined the British army straight from school, he left with neither money nor career. Not happy in India, they bought a 5,000-acre farm in Kenya and, armed with a book on farming, his father learned the job as he went along.

Gillinson reflects that in their different ways, his parents were both energetic and imaginative pioneers.

> "But with the rise of Mau Mau, the independence movement, life was getting ever more dangerous and they decided that my mother should return to England with my sister and me, where we both attended primary school. My father stayed in Kenya but not long after our return, my mother received a letter from him saying that he wanted to end their marriage. Simultaneously, my parents had to choose which school to send us to next and, since my mother had to earn a living playing the cello, they decided to send us to boarding school. Initially my father paid the school fees, but the deteriorating situation in Kenya soon rendered this impossible, so my mother applied for funding to cover our fees, and my sister and I were given scholarships so as not to undermine the continuity of our education."

Careers in music for a woman were quite difficult in Great Britain at that time; men got the best jobs, despite the fact that Gillinson's mother was a far better player than many of them. She subsequently advised her son that becoming a professional musician was a bad career choice, and that it would be better to establish a "real" career and enjoy music as an amateur. Despite the prejudice against women, she still managed to support herself and her children, and remained idealistically passionate about music until her dying day, practicing the cello daily through her 90th birthday. At first she wanted her son to play the piano; he began lessons at age 8 but demonstrated little interest or aptitude for it. He always knew that he wanted to play the cello, and from the moment he took it up at age 11 knew that he had found his love. "Life is all about what children love doing and seeing where that leads them," he reflects today. "Yet that can be the hardest thing to say to kids; they want certainty about their future, not a wide-open field of opportunities."

Once he returned from Africa, Gillinson's father became a reasonably successful businessman, but remained a frustrated artist at heart.

> "From a purely practical point of view, he wasn't part of developing my business mind or skills because I didn't see him much; we never established a close relationship, even after his return from Africa. I did find him interesting and extremely well read, with a challenging, questioning mind, but he had very low self-esteem that often came out in destructive ways with us kids. I'm sure that he wanted to be loving towards us, but he didn't know how. Much of the time my sister and I didn't like him because he fed our own insecurities. So much of life is action or reaction, and he was a large part of why I was determined to be as supportive as possible of my own kids."

The roots of Gillinson's father's lack of self-esteem were clear:

> "His parents told him repeatedly that they hadn't wanted a second child, that when he arrived he brought them bad luck and they had lost all their money. If angry, which was often, his mother would tell him that when she was pregnant with him she used to jump off chairs and take really hot baths to try to get rid of him. Only later in life did I fully comprehend what an unhappy person he was."

Self-Dependency & Entrepreneurial Skills

Gillinson lived through a far-from-typical experience, attending Frensham Heights—a UK progressive boarding school—for 11 years, from age 7 through 18. The school describes itself in broad-minded terms as part of a progressive movement to promote coed and less-formal relationships between teachers and students, with a wide range of clubs and extracurricular activities, while opposing all forms of racial, religious or social bigotry.

For many youngsters such a school would have been both fun and stimulating. Yet…

> "Initially it was sheer hell. I remember from the age of 7 crying myself to sleep—as did my sister—every night for some time. We found it shattering suddenly to be alone at that age, especially having been brought up on the farm where we saw our parents all the time and hardly ever saw any strangers. When people came to visit us on the farm in Kenya, it amused our parents that my sister and I would run and hide under the bed because we were so shy. However, the good thing in the longer term was that Frensham Heights toughened us up and enabled us to become independent. The school offered many strengths, central of which was seeking to nurture the development of the 'whole person.' Even though in those days Frensham was not at all demanding academically (most schools now have to be, no matter how progressive they are), they encouraged the arts, crafts and sports. As one fellow student said to me recently, 'Frensham prepared us for nothing and for everything!' In terms of supporting me with my cello studies, though, it was great, and they even brought in a cello teacher for me. It also became an exciting place to be, once I got over the initial loneliness. I started to think quite entrepreneurially, learning all sorts of skills that were definitely not on the curriculum, including how to pick locks, make treehouses and create invisible camps in the woods. Picking locks was one of the most important skills, as we regularly used to break into the school kitchen at night to make peanut butter sandwiches. That skill ended up proving useful for another reason. One of my biggest loves at school was carpentry and, for me, the carpentry teacher was by far the school's best and most inspirational. For my last major project, I built a chest of drawers and my mother had arranged a van to take it home. To our horror the carpentry building was locked, so I had to break in to collect my chest of drawers—no problem!"

Gillinson earned top marks in math and showed obvious talent in music, but Frensham Heights was a small school and he had little basis on which to compare or measure his musical progress. His transformational moment came when he was accepted into the National Youth Orchestra of Great Britain at age 16. He had become the star musician—admittedly among very few—at Frensham, but was still amazed to be accepted. At school he thought he was a terrific cellist, but upon arriving in the NYO was shocked to discover that everyone around him was either as good or better—the best players in the country.

> "At that time I was very insecure—fighting for an identity—but also intellectually arrogant: an unhelpful and contradictory combination. In such a small school my horizons were remarkably narrow, and here I was, surrounded by brilliant, excited, hugely talented peers, where every moment was pervaded by an overwhelming sense of optimism and idealism. A situation like that is transformative, and you either get demoralised or incredibly inspired; for me it was the latter. Everyone lifted everybody else's standards; we were all so excited about what we were creating together, as well as interacting with and learning from each other. To this day, the NYO remains one of the most inspirational experiences of my entire life. I still vividly remember my first full rehearsal with the orchestra, enveloped by this unimaginably wonderful sound. I was so overcome with emotion that I was unable to play a note for some time, as the tears ran down my cheeks. To this day, Brahms' Second Symphony, the first piece we played, remains hugely emotive for me."

Shyness & Competitiveness

At Frensham, Gillinson had remained shy and lacking in self-confidence. Despite his talents for music, math and carpentry, along with his growing entrepreneurial skills and imagination, he risked nothing in front of others. Part of the shyness doubtless remained from his early childhood on the Kenyan farm, rarely meeting new people. However, this progressive boarding school played a key role in developing his ability to look at situations without a fixed or prescribed framework.

> "We were often left to our own devices, which was terrific for developing creativity and exploring ideas, but useless in terms of getting qualifications for going to Oxford or Cambridge. Only much later did I realise that it had taught me a lot of very important, albeit less tangible life skills, despite for a long time thinking that I had learnt absolutely nothing of value there."

Coming toward the end of his time at Frensham, he very much wanted to go to Cambridge University, as that was the best place to study math. In addition, this was the planned destination and subject for a number of his NYO friends. Because Frensham had not covered large swathes of the syllabus needed for the entrance exam, his mother got him a math coach.

> "The tutor said that I was very talented at maths but that there wasn't a hope of my getting into Cambridge, because Frensham hadn't covered a large part of the necessary curriculum. His counterintuitive recommendation was that I try for a scholarship, hoping that I might get lucky with questions that I had covered, either at school or in the short time with him. I took the scholarship exam and hadn't been taught a single one of the questions on the paper, a totally humiliating experience."

Instead, Gillinson ended up going to London University to study math, applying to and entering Queen Mary College, attracted by their strong commitment to music. His need to prove himself, however, fed his competitiveness, with math and music the vehicles for validation. He also came from roots where, in altogether different ways, both his mother and father were driven. He realized very quickly that he had made a mistake in choosing math and that music had to be his life, so he left Queen Mary College and entered the Royal Academy of Music the following year, where he earned a Recital Diploma and won the top cello prize. He loved his four years there, having found his calling. Despite for the first time starting to gain some confidence through his cello playing, he continued to be relatively reclusive, burying himself in cello practice and reading. Everything was about wanting to be a great player. Engaging with people, which he found so much harder, came a distant second. Practicing cello as a boy gave him a foretaste of self-worth, among the first of a series of small bricks in building self-assurance, and this continued to grow, albeit slowly, in his time at the Royal Academy of Music.

Whether in the arts, sports, the sciences or so many other fields and pursuits, Gillinson feels that today's youth can and should work to inspire one another through sharing their learning; many of the programs that he later instituted directly support this ideal. His experience in the NYO bred humility, by being part of such an extraordinary group of players. And while not immediately apparent, those years also began to develop in him a keen sense of collaboration, of partnership, of looking beyond himself—traits from which the reclusive Gillinson had previously shied away.

Tools of the Trade

Carpentry also became an important part of his life, borne of his years at Frensham. As time went by it became a serious hobby. "When I married my first wife, at the age of 21, we bought a small Victorian worker's cottage, which consisted of not much more than the four walls. I built everything into the house: wardrobes, sideboards, bookshelves, the works. I loved it." At that time, there was a small antique shop near where they lived and he used to go in almost every day, talking to the owner, asking questions and developing a warm friendship. He learned more and more, then began buying 19th-century English furniture. Years later, when Gillinson and his second wife, a fashion buyer, realized that their lives were perpetually heading off in different directions, they decided that—for the marriage to work—they needed to do something together. They agreed to start a business, all the while investing any spare money in antique furniture. It eventually dawned on them that their business was sitting right in front of them, with the antiques that were relentlessly taking over their living room. His wife worked in the shop and did the selling, and Gillinson did the buying and restoration; he would often come back from an LSO evening concert and head into the shop to work on the furniture. "Carpentry became a love for me because of an inspirational teacher at school. I loved working with my hands, building things, exploring physical craftsmanship, finding creative solutions—a love that I carry to this day."

As someone who loves building things, creating lasting structures and working on the other side of the stage, the closest that Gillinson could ever come to being an ivory-tower manager would be if he actually built the tower in collaboration with his team....

1

Questions over Answers

Gillinson has always loved to learn, particularly through reading and math, because of his fascination with puzzles, of thinking things through, of asking questions, of analyzing.

"One of the inspiring things about management is that making one plus one equal two has absolutely no value, and would make the job as boring as I mistakenly assumed it would be when I was a cellist. My love of maths has been very useful in understanding structure and discipline, on which creativity almost always has to be built. In every meeting our team seeks to think laterally, looking for unusual ways to approach each issue, seeking hidden synergies. One of my mantras is that questions are more important than answers, and without them the chances of finding the best answers are minimal. Studying maths and music directly develops not only black-and-white analytical skills, but also an analytical attitude. Great performers must spend countless hours mastering the technical side of their instrument; only then are the notes liberated from the page to enable creative music-making. A mathematician learns to question every problem, to break each into retraceable component parts through critical thinking, testing and retesting. Reasoning and data become inextricably linked, regardless of whether the problem involves differential equations or how to bring music education to hundreds of thousands of young people. Teaching students to ask perceptive questions stokes the kind of thinking and reasoning skills that will serve them throughout their lives."

Make Just One Change: Teach Students to Ask Their Own Questions by Dan Rothstein and Luz Santana (Harvard Education Press, 2011), reveals the enormous learning and motivational benefits of being able to ask discerning questions as part of the educational process. Yet many classrooms do not promote that kind of thinking, frequently leading to commonplace results and flat learning curves.

Vulnerability & Possibilities

Gillinson aspires to avoid routines and believes that people should never allow themselves or their employees to become comfortable.

> "I always try to embrace new ideas, to challenge current thinking, to enjoy feeling vulnerable in the wake of thoughts that may not mesh with my own. But our meetings would not go anywhere if I thought I knew it all—we'd miss out on an infinite number of possibilities."

Gillinson tries to listen more than he talks, seeking to understand others' perspectives before attempting to have them understand his. He looks to give credit where due, and the resulting freedom and fellowship inspire far more security and creativity than the alternative. He also seeks to cultivate frankness in all relationships; bona fide trust is impossible without it.

An open mind by definition means a desire to uncover new opportunities, to take different avenues in confronting inevitable challenges, without being deterred when an initiative does not take off. Rowland Hussey Macy tried seven times before his Manhattan store became a hit. Hank Aaron went 0 for 5 in his first game with the Milwaukee Braves. Charles Schultz's high-school yearbook staff rejected every one of his cartoons. Jerry Seinfeld froze onstage during his first comedy club gig and was quickly jeered offstage. A reporter asked Pablo Casals, "Mr. Casals, you are 95 and the greatest cellist who ever lived. Why do you still practice six hours a day?" His reply? "Because I think I'm making progress."

The Heart of Questions

"Judge a man by his questions rather than by his answers." Voltaire said these words nearly 300 years ago, applicable just as much today. As much as we may wish differently, fundamental human issues rarely change with time. Gillinson learned one of the most important lessons of his life at the start of his time managing the London Symphony Orchestra. Knowing absolutely nothing about management and walking into a disastrous financial situation, he had no idea what the problems were, let alone how to address them. Neither did anyone else:

Clive Gillinson

"It was a really scary time and I spent countless sleepless nights trying to work out what we should do. Everything was continually churning in my head and initially none of us had any idea how to solve the immense problems we faced. All we could do was to analyse every aspect of the business, ask every question we could think of, and then come up with the best possible answers based on what we'd learned. Slowly I gained confidence that we would find answers if we kept asking questions. At last I began to sleep! Nowadays I rarely lose sleep over problems, as I have faith that with a terrific team we will always find a way to solve them, even if they appear insoluble at the start. I also seek to employ staff who are not just the smartest we can find, but who have curiosity and ask questions—never those who think they know the answers. None of us knows all the answers, and we certainly don't if we haven't first asked questions."

At one point in his managerial career, Gillinson faced a major dilemma when his board was considering a significant project that he and his management team thought was a bad idea. They all agreed that Gillinson would have real problems if he took a negative approach to the project, since the chairman had strongly backed it. Gillinson therefore asked the chairman if it would be useful to come up with all the questions that they needed to answer if they were going to proceed, and he agreed. When Gillinson went back with the questions that he and his team had come up with, the chairman's response was: "We're not doing this project, are we?" Gillinson was thrilled with this demonstration of the power of questions, and greatly respected the chairman for listening to what the questions had laid bare.

The questions themselves made clear that the project was not a good idea, yet so many people had started from the answer. Far too many people proceed in this way. Superficially it may appear difficult to embrace a truly open, democratic culture. Some conductors, particularly those of the past, would feel that they had to be dictators in order to impose their will—likewise with many CEOs and others in leadership positions. Yet Gillinson makes clear the benefits of the opposite approach.

> "Leadership isn't about telling people what to do; it's about using the resources, skills, experience and knowledge of everyone involved. After all, members of my team all know more about their particular area than I do. If I don't actively use that resource, I'm wasting it and it's therefore highly improbable that we will come up with the best answers. That doesn't mean it's possible to come up with perfect answers, because perfection does not exist. It's also possible that in one month, six months, years, we will have acquired more knowledge and realise that there are more questions we need to ask, which we didn't know when we made our decision. We've always got to be willing to accept that if the known facts change, then we change."

Despite a very rough journey at times, Gillinson's determination—coupled with the support of his close colleagues—sustained his uncompromising commitment to cultural change at the LSO. He also intuitively recognized that, however aggressively some of the players resisted change, constituents must sense a genuine willingness to be heard with patience and understanding, a crucial tenet that cannot be faked. People come to appreciate that asking the questions over setting the answers tends to avoid surprises along the way, and helps to maintain transparency. It also provides the best chance of taking everyone along on major decisions.

This process of openness and mutual understanding is ongoing, and nothing is off the table. "It's not a silly question," observes author Jostein Gaardner, "if you can't answer it." Gillinson is constantly disappointed at how many people think that leadership is about answers.

"Frequently it is not possible to determine an answer right away, and there is nothing wrong with acknowledging that. I know I was just as bad in the beginning, thinking my job was to come up with the answers. I discovered the flaws in that approach early on. In a self-governing orchestra, as the players own the orchestra, you have to take them with you on all decisions. Often they would discuss an issue together and come back to tell me how they thought we should proceed. I'd respond by first asking the questions that I thought were relevant. One particular chairman used to get very upset, saying that I was overruling the players. I tried to make clear that this was not the case, that we should never make decisions until we had been as rigorous as possible about asking questions. The players ultimately embraced the process and we learned to work together as real partners."

Informational Lenses

Gillinson generally deals with pushback by disseminating information as widely and transparently as possible, to ensure that people are kept fully up to date—the only way they can make well-informed decisions.

"Many leaders don't communicate extensively, mistakenly thinking that information is power. I see it the other way round; the only way to make the best decisions is to involve everyone, sharing as much information with them as possible. Confidentiality should only be for those things that absolutely have to remain so, which is probably no more than one percent of all information. Openness should be a mindset. The only power that matters is getting the right things done, ideally with everyone arriving at the destination together, not telling others what to do."

Of the people whom he has greatly admired, Gillinson often thinks about conductor Sir Colin Davis, who was always open, ever seeking the players' ideas:

> "But that takes courage; lots of conductors feel much 'safer' telling the players what to do. It's the same in management, in the business world; leaders need to have the courage to be totally open with information, engaging their teams as widely as possible. It's the only way to come up with the best answers; although that may sound risky, it rarely is. Everybody wins."

Ian Martin

Ian Martin, a banker and chairman of the St. Luke's Centre Management Company (he and Gillinson spearheaded an historic Anglican church's conversion into LSO St. Luke's, the orchestra's vibrant community and music-education center), makes clear that Gillinson is always extremely well prepared.

> "Particularly when going into negotiations, you've really got to have the pitch for a project thoroughly worked out, what the questions are that others may ask, the resulting answers, and ensuring that everything is consistent. In terms of our project converting the church, we did as much as we could, but also had to rely on architects, engineers and a range of others when we didn't have the skills ourselves. Asking the right questions of all involved and

obtaining as much information as possible beforehand was central to completing what has become an extremely successful venue."

Michael Tilson Thomas

The celebrated musician and composer Michael Tilson Thomas, principal conductor of the London Symphony Orchestra from 1988 to 1995, observes that a big word with Gillinson is "relationship," which comes very much out of his work with the LSO:

"Clive always realized the importance of the orchestra's relationships with its members, supporters and patrons, between the government, its conductors… all of these various relationships that were essential for there to be a meaningful identity for an artistic ensemble, none of which can be taken for granted. There's always something to be done for the relationship to be nurtured. Working with a self-governing ensemble, where decisions are made by consensus, is inevitably tricky to balance. Clive has always been a champion of ideas being raised, even if at that moment they haven't a chance of going through. The fact that they were brought up and discussed allows them to be revisited at a later time, letting some of the more idealistic things eventually move forward. Chief among these, and on which so much of the LSO's identity is based, is its educational work—the creation of St. Luke's, for example, a wonderful and visionary idea that has stood the test of time. This was quite controversial when first presented, by no means a slam dunk for Clive to pull off. Many people questioned why we needed it."

Transformational Change

When he started managing the LSO, whose affairs were in disarray and financially perilous, Gillinson was clear that he had to transform its culture from one based on the orchestra serving the players to one in which the first question should always be, "What is best for the music?" He instinctively knew that, in the end, success would follow. The pervasive LSO culture of self-interest was rooted in the founding of an ensemble run and managed by and for the players. Gillinson had to persuade them of the need for change. He knew that he would have to persuade them to take this on trust and, simultaneously, that he had to earn that trust, since there was no way to prove in advance that his philosophy would work.

> "When I set out to transform the LSO's culture, I had to find partners amongst the players who felt the same way as I did, because there's no hope of achieving transformational cultural change on one's own. I sought and found players who shared my vision, and gradually this core group grew, enabling us to encourage an ongoing conversation about long-term objectives and cultural change, and how these would be fundamental to achieving the best for the music and the orchestra, as well as the players. It's natural for people not to accept the need for change at face value. Initially, many of the players fought ferociously to resist me, because all they could see was what they were going to lose. I could not yet prove what they were going to win; all I could do was to make the best possible case for it. A number of the orchestra meetings in those early days were very unpleasant, with some players being extremely aggressive, fighting for the status quo and their own short-term self-interest. I knew, however, that I had to maintain my cool, even though I often went home afterwards feeling very low and occasionally on the verge of tears."

Gillinson was clear with them that the orchestra would only move forward through an act of faith, but that if they did commit to always putting the quality of music-making first, everything else would follow: the greatest conductors, soloists, tours, recordings, TV and financial support. "Despite much initial kicking and screaming, more and more of the players started to buy into this vision, aided by the fact that we began to achieve incremental successes."

The problems emanated from how easy it was for players to see only their potential losses; the upside was not immediately visible, as it had not yet happened. Gillinson also had to accept that it would not be possible to persuade everyone, and that his job was to convince enough of them to enable the momentum to carry the rest. "Changing culture takes years, and I genuinely think it's the hardest thing to achieve in management. This is particularly true with self-serving cultures, such as the LSO's at that time."

Gillinson has observed that company culture is largely self-perpetuating. This was demonstrated at the LSO when they started to attract a different sort of player, drawn by their clearly enunciated ambition to put the music first. These were players who would not have been attracted to join the orchestra before the change. In addition, some of those who did not buy into the new culture left, no longer feeling that the LSO was their home. The moment that Gillinson knew the orchestra's culture had fundamentally changed came a number of years later, after two particular concerts the LSO performed at the Barbican Centre.

"The second concert was a straight repeat of the first and was noticeably less good. I raised this at our next players meeting and asked why they thought this had happened. After an extensive discussion, someone suggested that there had been no rehearsal of any sort before the second concert, so perhaps not everyone's head was totally in the music before the concert began. After much discussion, they themselves decided that we would never again do a repeat concert of any kind without at least a brief rehearsal before the performance, even on tour where the same programme is often repeated many times. This was a decision purely based on what was best for the music, as no one would receive any additional money for doing it. For me it was a pivotal moment, encapsulating all that we had been seeking to achieve."

When he first came to Carnegie Hall, Gillinson likewise did not expect the staff and board to trust him from day one; as with the LSO players, he knew that he had to earn their trust. Was it Carnegie Hall's place, for example, to establish citywide, cross-cultural festivals or create a fellowship program for the finest post-graduate musicians in the US, training them in education and community-engagement skills that would enable them to transform lives through music throughout their careers? He would ask, "How can we have a transformational impact on music standards in the USA? How do we work to ensure that every child has access to great music? What are the needs of society, where are the problems, and is there any way that we can help address those through music?" He never looked at the answers first, recognizing that the staff and board work as a team, with so many ideas coming through them.

At the LSO, Gillinson found that the orchestra's members largely focused on their lives as players:

> "They'd of course ask questions and come up with ideas, but orchestral players generally don't feel that their day-to-day lives are creative. An irony that struck me early on in my LSO days was that the musicians do not generally function as individuals per se, but as an inseparable part of an extraordinarily skillful team; they're rarely able to challenge and test things as individuals within that group. However, the administrative team, even down to relatively junior positions, had more freedom to be individually creative than most of the players."

The same is naturally true at Carnegie Hall; team members function as creative individuals while utterly devoted to the overarching goals, and management actively tries to ensure that there is space for everyone's ideas.

This kind of creativity must remain aligned with long-term goals. Joel Klein, former chancellor of the New York City Department of Education, worked with Gillinson and the Juilliard School's President Joseph Polisi to create Ensemble Connect (originally called The Academy, then Ensemble ACJW), a two-year fellowship program for the finest young professional classical musicians that equips the fellows to develop musical careers encompassing great performance together with teaching, community engagement, advocacy, entrepreneurship and leadership. In his early conversations with Gillinson in establishing The Academy, Klein's sense was that there were many members of the cultural community and others who were eager to work with the schools on arts and music programs, an opportunity for them to increase their cash flow and bring in resources. He was concerned about the coherence and sustainability of many of these initiatives, that what they did should not be a one-off event but needed to be well thought through.

> "Clive's proposal fit quite well with my thinking and we worked closely together for eight years. He was always very interested to know

Joel Klein

what we needed in the schools, asking perceptive questions then seeing how that could be accomplished. Cultural organizations bring value to schools, but very few of them really want to focus on how we create the kind of sustained, meaningful engagement for kids with the arts. Clive always tried to see things through my lens—to listen, ask and learn from my experience and perspective as chancellor, then come back to me with ideas about what made sense from what we were trying to accomplish, and to do it in a meaningful way. Ensemble Connect is a key example of that, in bringing unique talent and opportunities to students to which they would not otherwise be exposed. Intellectual acumen, integrity and creativity are qualities that we'd like to see in everyone. Clive was constantly challenging me to think harder, to think better. I'll never forget early on when we were sitting down together talking about the arts, and I asked him when we're recruiting teachers how to know which are the right ones with the right set of skills. He was just as thoughtful and engaged on something like that, which led me to know that I was working with someone who not only thought big but thought well."

For his part, Polisi reflects on Gillinson's vision:

"I can't think of another arts administrator who has the energy to keep addressing new ideas and multiples of what he's initially created, for example with the National Youth Orchestra of the USA: to start a younger orchestra is both admirable and striking. I use the term 'widening the circle.' The initial idea may come from the top, but in order to test it, to see if it's viable, you've got to constantly bring more colleagues into the circle, to hear their input, to discuss their questions, to see where adjustments could and should be made, so that finally you have a large-enough circle of supporters to reach critical mass to be able to move the project forward, often in multiple ways."

Joseph Polisi

Context & Direction

The staff at Carnegie Hall enjoys this kind of comprehensive and fluid exchange; that culture has been built over time by involving staff, asking questions on all sides and ensuring that ideas are embraced by the entire team. With trustees, however, it can be more complex. The staff are doing Carnegie Hall's work and living it every day of the week, whereas trustees are living their own lives, with Carnegie Hall's issues not necessarily front of mind most of the time. Suddenly they come to a board meeting and have to consider specific questions. There is a danger that they will not have the nuances, the subtleties, all of the context behind the issues being discussed. To address this challenge, Gillinson sends a monthly memo to the trustees (and weekly to the chairman, president, secretary and treasurer), so that they are aware of everything as it evolves. He will also cover topics the team is considering, leaving them as open situations for feedback. In addition, Gillinson meets individually with most of Carnegie Hall's trustees one or more times a year, to catch up and see if there are any issues that they would like to discuss personally, which they may be reticent to raise within the context of a board meeting. He firmly believes in the importance of keeping the dialogue going outside the boardroom as well as within it.

A central part of all effective management is keeping broader goals at the forefront, for both staff and trustees:

> "Organisations will always have short-term as well as long-term plans, but the fact is that every idea or project has to have a context as part of an overall strategy. No idea stands on its own. When you're the person running the organisation, you're the one responsible for retaining that big picture all the time. With the heads of departments, their lives revolve around their particular part of the entity. At Carnegie Hall we have a fantastic team, very imaginative, and—within a transparent environment—they will always ask important questions and raise essential issues for discussion. However, by definition it is not possible for them to live with the overview all the time, since their primary focus has to be on their own area of responsibility."

Jonathan Vaughan

Jonathan Vaughan, vice principal and director of music at the Guildhall School of Music & Drama and former director of the UK NYO, recognizes that questions are at the heart of everything Gillinson does.

"I first encountered Clive when he was managing director of the LSO and I was freelancing with them before becoming a member. From the first moments of hearing him speak, it was obvious that here was a former player who spoke the same language as the other players. His great strength was that he had been one of their number and knew what it meant to sit where they did. He brought about huge changes to the orchestra's culture, not because they always agreed with him (they frequently did not and there were some very heated debates in orchestral meetings), but because, at the heart of things, they trusted him. Once I became an LSO member and was able to attend their meetings, I found his intellect and logical argument inspiring. On a monthly basis he faced a sometimes hostile self-governing orchestra that could pitch any question without notice. He was extraordinarily adept at fielding them, preparing the ground for difficult conversations by dripping in information for weeks beforehand. Decisions were made and ultimately ratified because the orchestra had been fully informed of the landscape in which they operated and shown the alternatives. As a young player, I became so interested in Clive's view of the world that it seemed a natural step after five years of membership to join the board and an honour two years later to become its chairman. The insights and inspiration I gained during my tenure working alongside Clive are the reasons I wanted, and was able, to pursue my managerial career. He talks often about our ability to think we know all the answers to a problem, to allow our own supposition to fill in the gaps in our knowledge without questioning its legitimacy. We've all been in management courses talking about our 'inner rescuer' who thinks he knows the answers and produces solutions almost without thought. Clive's approach is far more rigorous; you spend an hour with him on a tough assignment and you feel like you've spent a week sitting an exam! The joy, of course, is that you may know the answers within yourself and just need him to ask the right questions. Even today if I get stuck on a problem I will often ask myself, *What questions would Clive ask about this?* and more often than not the answers emerge. He's also skilled at saying no to people. On more than one occasion I've heard him say, 'Would it be helpful if I make a list of the questions we need to answer if we are to go with your proposition?' The other party typically gets to about question three and realizes that the idea isn't going to fly."

Anthony Marx

Anthony Marx, president and CEO of the New York Public Library, relates: "Clive captures the rationale of Socrates in that being too sure of the answer is always going to lead to trouble. Decisions still need to be made, but it's best to get them right rather than *assume* they're right. Asking more is always going to lead to better outcomes."

2

Education & Engagement

Significant and established research shows that the arts are a fundamental part of developing every human individual, also enhancing learning in other areas. Eric Jensen, author of *Arts with the Brain in Mind* (ASCD, 2001), has extensively researched studies on the arts, learning and the brain, showing unequivocally that the arts are crucial to children's education and should be an integral part of school curricula on par with math, science, and language.

Gillinson recognized this from the beginning. In the mid-1990s, the political climate around arts funding in the UK led to education emerging as a critical element. Organizations suddenly had to deliver not only excellence in performance but also demonstrate social value and community engagement. Yet prior to this mandate he had already developed educational outreach programs in the late '80s and early '90s. Working with the likes of Peter Renshaw and Richard McNicol, Gillinson developed the LSO Discovery music-education program, so that when the Arts Council announced a stabilization fund for UK orchestras whose criteria included education and access, the LSO had all the pieces in play and was well prepared to take full advantage of it.

Amid the larger debate about where education should be heading overall, and the perennial budgetary constraints that particularly affect arts and cultural education, Gillinson sees a key part of Carnegie Hall's role as seeking to play a dynamic part in music education and opportunities for engagement with, and access to, music—in New York City, nationally and internationally. Education lies at the core of its mission, and central to his philosophy is that, in most cases, Carnegie Hall should give away its educational resources, both to other music organizations and to individuals.

Many people and organizations look at their arts-education programs and ask how to monetize them. "We are frequently asked that question," Gillinson acknowledges, "yet in my view it's not the right question. Yes, there are times when it can be relevant, but in general it's about enabling the right things to happen, using partnerships to broaden access and opportunity." For years Carnegie Hall has raised the money to give away Link Up, their multi-year sequential program for elementary-school children, and each year the number of orchestras served across the country has increased. They now share it with 90 orchestras, training both them and local teachers to deliver it, thus enabling the program to reach about 380,000 kids a year at an annual cost to Carnegie Hall of approximately $750,000. This leverage is massive, achieving benefits for the lives of the kids who are involved in the program that neither the orchestras nor Carnegie Hall could ever achieve alone.

Carnegie Hall wanted to expand this program yet further, but did not have the resources to do so. In a vindication of Gillinson's belief that money follows vision, they successfully sought a major donation in 2015 that will enable them to expand the program's reach to five million students over the next 10 years. That leverage and reach would not have been possible had Carnegie Hall not been giving away the program—a central part of what inspired the donor. Giving it away enables smaller-budget orchestras to deliver world-class educational resources that they could never develop alone, in the process not only playing a crucial role in the lives of the students they reach, but also in the future of music and success of the orchestras themselves. Most organizations would not spend $750,000 a year on such a concept, even if they had it, yet a look at the math shows the cost at around $2 a child. Carnegie Hall actively seeks these sorts of partnerships, to maximize the benefit of everything it does.

Such donors and partnerships are key, given the huge gulf between publicly funded systems such as in Europe, and the largely philanthropic model in the US. Officials responsible for distributing public funding to the arts rarely lose their jobs by playing it safe and seeking to avoid mistakes. However, if they take risks by promoting enterprising and exciting projects that subsequently fail, they are likely to find themselves headed for the exit. Because little public money exists for programming in the US, Gillinson acknowledges that most support comes through individuals whom they have to excite about their vision and ideas:

> "If you excite a public funding body, they frequently get scared; if you excite an individual donor, sponsor or foundation, there's a real chance they'll back you. It is rare to find a philanthropist who gets excited about safe, comfortable ideas! One of the strengths of the US funding system is that it effectively reinforces what we should in any case always demand of ourselves: to seek the extraordinary in everything we do."

Gillinson knows that Carnegie Hall alone cannot change music education in the US. It can, however, ensure that the arts—music in particular—are a life-changing part of the lives of the children it reaches. In addition, by seeing Carnegie Hall as a resource that supports the future of music and helps to ensure the success of others, it can play a crucial national role in developing access to and engagement with music.

Indispensable Teaching

Parents and administrators love what Carnegie Hall is doing and highly value it, yet "no single organisation can change the world," Gillinson reflects.

> "But if all of us understood that we're part of an ecology that can help to do so, much more could happen. On a positive note, ever-increasing numbers of organisations see it as a central part of their responsibility to create access to and engagement with the arts, and are now addressing this opportunity gap."

He also thinks that those who view this kind of work as audience development miss the point:

> "A program like Link Up would be judged as a disastrous audience-development project, because the students we reach are all around the US. Most of them can't get to Carnegie Hall and may never do so. Yes, over the long term it's surely developing audiences, but we do not see the fact that most of these audiences may never come to Carnegie Hall as a failure. Our mission is not to serve the institution, but for the institution to serve the future of music and thereby enhance people's lives."

Link Up is an extraordinary program that offers communities and schools a wide array of practical and engaging materials, from teacher guides to student and concert components, just one in a bevy of impactful educational programs developed by Carnegie Hall's Weill Music Institute. Gillinson's desire to look outward was actively fed from his time managing the London Symphony Orchestra, where he developed a consistent focus on education and widening access. He and Sanford I. Weill—chairman of Carnegie Hall for 24 years and now its president—share a passion for making music part of the lives of as many kids as possible.

Gillinson and Sanford Weill

The legendary soprano Jessye Norman makes clear that education is key and has seen first-hand how seriously Gillinson takes this:

"The Weill Music Institute thrives through its own mission, that education in the arts is its own reward. Young people need special care, and America's very first nationwide youth orchestra came into being because of Clive's vision and knowledge. Having been an orchestral musician himself, he understands that young players need a place to learn the language of ensemble music-making and how such experiences can infuse and imbue their solo playing."

In reflecting on young people and careers, Gillinson fondly shares this anecdote involving Leonard Bernstein and one of Norman's experiences in establishing herself:

"Harry Kraut, Leonard Bernstein's manager, told me about the time he convinced Lenny to audition Jessye Norman. This was before her meteoric rise to fame, so at that time she was unknown to him. He was really tired and didn't want to do the audition and asked Harry to cancel it, but Harry said it was too late as she'd travelled specially to sing for him. Lenny reluctantly agreed to see it through. When she arrived, he asked her to sing a number of specific pieces and she made it clear that she was only willing to sing the music that she had prepared. When she'd sung it all, he was so overwhelmed by her singing that he asked her to sing something further; she apologised and said she didn't have anything further prepared. He then asked her to stay and talk for a while. However, she apologised again and said she had to leave since she had a train to catch. As she left, he turned to Harry and said, 'Who is that incredible woman?' She became one of his favourite soloists."

Jessye Norman

The eminent pianist Emanuel Ax, in common with Norman and many of today's major artists, is eager to see far less of a gap between the stage and classroom:

"When I was a kid, pretty much everybody took music lessons, because it was one of the few extracurricular things to do. Today, with the technological developments, there's just so much choice, so many other ways of doing things with kids, and I get the feeling that we musicians are becoming more and more of a rarity within the educational scheme of things. We're looking to change that. I think I could help out with music teachers, and would like to get to know them in the New York public school system. Clive and I have long talked about creating a major prize for great educators, which it looks like will happen. We need to put educational talent on the same level as musical talent. I would venture to guess that for every great teacher, especially with kids, I could name 10 marvelous pianists. It's not so easy to find great teachers; we need to attract bigger talent to this area. We should make it more financially attractive, and make sure that well-known musicians emphasize the educational aspect, meeting with teachers to make sure they feel they're valued while encouraging more young people to go into teaching. There's an incredible talent pool for performers nowadays, in Asia for example, so we're getting such fantastic instrumentalists. If we could find a way to make teaching just as attractive, and not just related to music, how wonderful that would be. Really talented teachers are some of the most remarkable people in the world and we just don't emphasize that enough."

Emanuel Ax

Most politicians' talking points are filled with how important our families—our children—are, but beyond parents, who deals with children each day? Teachers. "We don't seem to make that jump," Ax observes wistfully, "either in terms of remuneration, respect or support. That's one of the things that Clive's trying to look at, to change."

While running the LSO, Gillinson worked with Bernstein, Kraut and Michael Tilson Thomas to launch the Pacific Music Festival in 1990, a Tanglewood summer music-camp concept for Japan. Gillinson recalls those days:

"When Lenny arrived, it was clear he was very ill, although we didn't realise until later that he'd already been receiving chemotherapy for lung cancer. He had a doctor and acupuncturist with him. When we saw how sick he was, I and others pressed him to go home for treatment, but he was absolutely clear that under no circumstances would he let the students down. Before every rehearsal the acupuncturist would work with him to reduce the pain, so that he could undertake the rehearsals and, as always, his music-making was hugely inspiring. Come the first concert, it was heartbreaking to watch him backstage, struggling even to be able to get up and move. However, once on the podium, he gave everything and conducted a series of remarkable concerts. It was shocking to watch him on the platform looking totally full of life and utterly engaged, then the minute he was backstage, the life would drain out of him and he would have to lay down to recover. At the press conference that launched the festival, he talked about what had been the most important aspect of his life: conductor, pianist, composer or teacher? He said that by far the most important for him was to make sure that all he had learned from his extraordinary teachers, like Serge Koussevitsky, should be passed on to the next generation. He was clear that what he felt most proud about in his whole career was his role as a teacher. One thing that never fails to thrill me is that even now, so many years after his death, hardly a day passes without somebody saying to me that the reason they fell in love with music was because of Leonard Bernstein, especially through his Young People's Concerts. Astonishing that one person could be among the greatest conductors who ever lived, write *West Side Story* (to me the greatest musical ever written), and be the greatest music teacher anybody of our generation has ever experienced, not to mention a very fine and versatile pianist."

Despite Bernstein's indelible example, the realization that music education is for everyone has been a painfully slow process to put into widespread practice. Ian Martin retains palpable gratitude:

"Clive not only has credibility, but he always firmly believed and was able to tell that music is for everyone. That's driven him, which is quite unusual as organisations are typically thinking of their own particular group of interested customers, clients or audiences. Clive would like the whole world to be able to play and engage with music if he could. A generation ago, very few people shared the concept and vision of taking music to the wider context of schools and local communities. Whereas previously it was elitist, nowadays there's very much a link from the street on one end to the concert hall on the other. People are interacting much more, creating all kinds of amazing opportunities to become involved."

Access to the arts is better these days in a city like New York, yet it obviously remains quite unequal. Issues of equity persist, with communities of poverty not getting exposure to the arts and culture. Joel Klein closely considered and worked to address this reality for many years.

"Those issues of equity were very big on my agenda, and working with institutions like Carnegie Hall clearly made things better, though there's still a long way to go. Our educational standards are far too low; we're so afraid to establish the standards that our students really need. It's a much different world than when I grew up. Sticking with Common Core—the state standards initiative—is good, so that at a minimum kids are ready for college. In some cases, though, a greater focus on acquiring knowledge got lost in the establishment. Schools want kids to think big thoughts and so forth, but doing that without grounding them in history, science, the arts… these are really valuable and we've lost some of that."

Filling the Gaps

Other institutions have also stepped in to help rectify what schools do not provide. New York's Museum of Modern Art, for example, made a decision on the cusp of the 21st century that, while interested in connecting with children of all ages, teenagers are where they want to concentrate; they are more independent and likely to continue their engagement with the museum after they go to college and make their way in the world, rather than 8- or 9-year-old children whose interests are much less formed. MoMA puts forth a full range of programming for teenagers, whether from public or private schools, from disadvantaged or wealthier parts of the city; their goal is to make the museum the place they think about when considering art. In a way, museums stepped into the breach left by the public schools' abandoning the arts in the late '60s, and the programs collectively offered by museums are astounding.

Glenn Lowry

Glenn Lowry, an art historian and MoMA's director since 1995, has closely witnessed this educational decline:

"We often work with schools and private enterprise seeking to fill the gaps left by curriculum changes, which doesn't mean that we're fully able to do so, because we're not. It isn't a real substitute. It's not at all because superintendents, principals and teachers aren't sensitive to this issue; they are. It's purely a matter of funding and volition. When parents demand that their children be well educated, realizing that this includes the arts and humanities as much as the sciences, then it will happen. But so long as parents aren't slamming their fists on the table, saying 'I want my child to understand the visual arts as much as she understands math,' then the dial is not going to move. We can talk as much as we want that being aware of the arts is an essential part of being human, but that's not going to force the system to address what's now an almost 50-year-old problem. In the end it's all about resources. I've probably talked to every school superintendent in the area since I've been here, and there's not been a single one who hasn't been sympathetic to the problem. But they're also bound into a system that gives them very little latitude, because it's so woefully underfunded. As a society, we're into skills-based testing and also looking collectively at what it takes to get into a university, which themselves are cutting back on the humanities—all of which make for a system-wide problem. Yet when people make decisions to pursue careers in the humanities, they're fulfilled, they're happy. It's an essential part of how we think and learn. And while not optimistic that the system will change anytime soon, I do see multiple ways for curious children to obtain the knowledge they need. They just need to work twice as hard!"

As these children grow and begin choosing colleges and careers, some will decide to pursue the performing arts, applying to places such as Juilliard, Curtis, Berklee College of Music, New England Conservatory and Cleveland Institute of Music. In an encouraging sign of the benefits of a flexible and well-rounded education, the focus of these institutions is not exclusively on preparing the next great instrumental soloist or elite orchestral player. Joseph Polisi has always taken a pragmatic approach, yielding consistent and far-reaching benefits:

"What we do is to educate and prepare students, not necessarily for solo or orchestral careers, but to address a wide panoply of opportunities within the performing-arts arena, from which they'll then figure out how to use them in forming their own careers. We don't want them to put all their eggs in one basket, but to have them think as broadly as possible. Many of the young artists whom we see become very involved in things like artist-teaching find them so fulfilling. The old paradigm of going to a place like Juilliard, Curtis and others, then making a solo or orchestral career, goes back to the 1940s and '50s and no longer exists. The curriculum is now designed to prepare these students for broad-based careers, so they know what the significant opportunities as cultural entrepreneurs are all about."

The celebrated mezzo-soprano Joyce DiDonato well understands that such initiatives must happen:

"Our students *need* the arts in the curriculum, and Carnegie Hall deserves applause for having a leader at the helm who is working tirelessly to achieve this. Not only does music combine all other learning disciplines (language, math, reading, physical), but perhaps most importantly, it can still teach empathy—a trait I feel we need more and more of, but is not being nurtured. Through music we travel through time, through history, through cultures, and begin to see that we are connected to each other in a unique and powerful way. It unifies. It calls us to action. It heals wounds. I recognize that I'm a chronic optimist, yet I believe it helps each of us make better sense of the world."

Joyce DiDonato

Open Doors

Thanks to such curricula, and the integration of cultural entrepreneurship that—in preparation and scope—goes far beyond collecting a paycheck for a performance engagement, today's young artists have a much better sense of the societal environment they will be entering. Polisi and Juilliard, for example, knew that they wanted these young artists to go into New York City public schools, and approached the city's Department of Education, which was quite receptive and helped financially and logistically. The Ensemble Connect fellowship program, jointly created by Carnegie Hall and Juilliard, adds a further dimension to this focus on outreach, and has developed a very close relationship with the New York City public school system. "You don't need an enormous level of resources," Polisi explains.

"What you do need is a serious teaching institution, an artistic organization such as an arts center or orchestra, and a city's department of education. It just takes the spirit to get it going, which is where Clive and I came in. We pushed it quite hard with our own institutions and then externally. It's obviously a win-win as it both aligns with our mission and doesn't stretch resources too thin. It's always been our hope that this program would be replicated around the country, but sadly that's not yet happened."

Throughout each season, these young artists—part of Ensemble Connect— not only work in the New York City public school system, but also go out into the community, working in nontraditional venues and with people coping with challenging circumstances in healthcare, correctional and senior-service facilities.

Many people have no idea about the extent of their talents. In Gillinson's case, shyness meant that he limited his horizons for some time. This also effectively worked against his achieving what he sought: success and self-esteem. True engagement and finding his place came well after college, in yet another sign for young people to be careful of preconceived educational and career ideas that offer little more space than a prescription pad:

"People succeed when they're not thinking about themselves, but are committed to contributing to others' lives. Suddenly life opens up. That was the key to my own development. In management I found a vocation through which I could make a real contribution, where I was suddenly forced to interact, to constantly be involved with people, seeking to convince them to take journeys of exploration with us. My job involves people from morning till night—the best thing that could have happened to me. Concentrating on the job and not myself drew out bits of me that I didn't know existed and hadn't dreamt were there. In many ways I guess it's like being an actor, who can be shy as a person but, when given a role to hide behind, is able to project without inhibitions. The role of a manager is very similar. I had to go for it, talk to people, live the part, share our vision and engage people with it. In doing this I was no longer thinking of myself but of the mission, of serving people through music and education. Suddenly it became easy, as it involved communicating the things I'm passionate about."

In common with many managers and leaders, Gillinson is quite clear that it is vital for arts organizations to work within the education system, but that they cannot and should not seek to replace teachers:

"We can only do so much, since we almost never have overall responsibility for education, nor should we. However, we can work in the schools and be an active voice as part of wider conversations about where education needs to go. In doing this it is important that we never replace what the schools themselves should be doing, and that we are always complementary partners of the teachers with whom we work, enhancing the experiences they offer to their students while never reducing their responsibility."

Paul King

At the New York City Department of Education's Office of Arts and Special Projects, Executive Director Paul King is happy to share details of what he refers to as a kind of golden age in arts education:

"Our current mayor and chancellor are extremely committed to arts education. We have a $23 million annual allocation directly targeted at arts education. It's not just a purely conservatory approach but rather more youth development, the transfer of skills that come with music, dance, theater and arts education. Our best partners are really committed to thinking about the whole child. We have extremely gifted partners working with pre-K teachers and sites, developmentally appropriate for very young students, as well as those who help us with college and career preparation—there's a shared sense of responsibility with the DoE and our partners as far as how we make that happen. We're so fortunate in New York to have a huge array of over 450 different arts organization with which we work, both large and small, doing extraordinary and innovative community work, including expanding our involvement in film and media. With 1700 schools there's really a place at the table for everyone. Mayor DeBlasio and the Department of Cultural Affairs are really keen on supporting the smaller community-based organizations. It's great to have partners with a national profile and citywide reach, such as Carnegie Hall, and also extremely important to have the locally centered groups as well, including organizations with the expertise to take on the role of how to address the arts for special-needs populations."

In terms of personal-development and career steps beyond the crucial elements of arts education, Gillinson loves the fact that so many young people want to meet with him to talk about their careers. One of his policies is to keep an open door for anyone who wants to discuss career ideas and options. He is among a large number of successful individuals who look outward in this way (though unfortunately many still do not).

"Otherwise we're not doing our best to ensure that people at least have the chance to fulfill their potential. If each person were able to align his or her talents with their job, we'd have a much happier world. I'm not interested in giving advice or telling anybody what to do, because then it's about me and not them. I also don't think of it as mentoring per se, but providing a supportive sounding board to enable people to seek their own answers. If you've sown the seeds— about education, personal fulfillment and looking outward with curiosity, rigour and commitment, this at least gives them the best possible chance of finding their own ideal path."

3

Journeys of Curiosity & Discovery

The arts can play a key role in stimulating curiosity, enabling both children and adults to continue to grow and develop throughout their lives. The Arts and Passion-Driven Learning Institute—led by the Harvard University Graduate School of Education and the Silk Road Project (initiated by the cellist Yo-Yo Ma in 1998 to encourage collaboration between artists and institutions)—is among countless high-profile programs and studies that regularly confirm the multifaceted benefits of ongoing exposure to—and participation in—the arts. Children have innate curiosity, yet many adults do not. Where does it go? "I've been very fortunate in having Yo-Yo Ma as a friend for over 40 years, who's the most curious person I know," Emanuel Ax reflects, yet asks the key question: "Kids have such curiosity to begin with, but what as a society are we doing with that?"

So much of education is linear, with single-answer questions. "This stifles creativity instead of teaching young people how to ask questions, how to explore ideas," Gillinson observes.

> "Kids who come up with several possible answers may well do poorly in exams and are often considered to be a nuisance in the classroom, but they are the ones we need to nurture. As long as they retain that curiosity, their lives will be far more interesting and fulfilling, and they will contribute so much more to the lives of others. The fact is that there are no right answers in music and the arts, which are about exploring and searching for truth, understanding, insight, beauty, inspiration. It's a philosophy of life. Technically, of course, there are many skills that need to be learned, but when exploring the art itself, rather than the technique, there is no such thing as linear."

Nurturing Individuals...

The celebrated French conductor and composer Pierre Boulez once said that without curiosity we die. Einstein cast a different but equally powerful light: "Imagination is far more important than knowledge." Such statements cannot help but make an indelible impression on students from any background. "To imagine there's only a single answer to every question discourages kids from exploring alternatives, and is likely to suppress their innate curiosity and the development of their imagination," Gillinson confirms.

> "The most creative kids want to explore. I'm always fascinated by the fact that you hardly ever meet a child who isn't curious. What a tragic irony that education frequently knocks the creativity out of them, when it should be nurtured."

Carnegie Hall's education programs are structured to give individuals the opportunity to contribute, to challenge them to be collaborative participants rather than recipients of knowledge, information or data. Every project is about engaging and fostering the curiosity that already abundantly exists in children. This is not something that schools or teachers have to create, but they certainly have a responsibility to cultivate it.

Paul King observes:

> "One of the things Clive always says is that if it's a really good, exciting idea, then it's eminently fundable, a case where having a keen sense of curiosity and discovery come together with a pragmatic way of being supported. I think about things that Carnegie Hall has done, such as the National Youth Orchestra—Clive was really curious about a national culture that would support and highlight young musicians, an example of something that hadn't existed before and that took a huge amount of work to set up and program: auditioning kids, bringing them to New York City, going on international tours.... Then that led to the question, 'So what do you do with those kids who aren't quite ready for a national youth orchestra?' Thus NYO2 was born. It comes out of a genuine sense of curiosity and care."

Four years after creating the National Youth Orchestra of the USA, Carnegie Hall's Weill Music Institute launched NYO2, a free two-week training program for American instrumentalists aged 14–17, in partnership with The Philadelphia

Orchestra, a longtime Carnegie Hall partner. Allison Vulgamore, the Orchestra's president and CEO, shares how it came about and what it has been like working with both the Weill Music Institute and Carnegie Hall itself:

> "Clive spoke to me about the NYO2 concept, which the Weill Music Institute team had developed, to see if we might want to explore expanding our partnership in this way. It's been very special working with WMI and fun that Sarah Johnson—its director—was once here at The Philadelphia Orchestra. I find the WMI staff to be deeply dedicated and open to joint programming and planning, all of which have been the focus of the NYO2 residency. I also find the depth of their staff and the capabilities they are making possible an extraordinary example."

NYO2 is focused on attracting talented students from groups underserved by and underrepresented in the classical orchestral field. Vulgamore has closely considered what this means and how to reach these groups:

> "These communities have been very much at the forefront of The Philadelphia Orchestra's mind. We have our own local partnerships that are facilitated by our collaborative learning department. We've been spreading the word through our work with Settlement Music School here in Philadelphia—the country's largest and oldest community school of the arts. We also have a new and growing artistic partner with the All City Orchestra from the public school system. When we first discussed the idea, the coaching was to be in Purchase, New York, with side-by-side concerts to happen in the subsequent season in New York City; I asked if we could complement that by bringing NYO2 to Philadelphia."

Vulgamore reflects on The Philadelphia Orchestra's longstanding relationship with Carnegie Hall, where it performs an annual series:

> "We were one of the first orchestras to perform regularly at Carnegie Hall, from great concerts and music directors to Jack Benny, with whom we also performed in the early days. The musicians have been phenomenally supportive and enthusiastic about expanding our relationship with Carnegie Hall, such a natural connection, with

nearly a third of the orchestra signed up to participate in NYO2's intensive 10-day training period in New York."

Allison Vulgamore

After a comprehensive communications and recruitment process, Carnegie Hall received some 800 letters of recommendation and all concerned found the numbers exceedingly encouraging.

Young people have consistently demonstrated a love and hunger for classical music once exposed to it, yet so often that basic element does not come into play. Beyond becoming tomorrow's audiences, their musical training has been universally shown to engender a host of developmental positives that carry throughout life. Vulgamore reflects on how projects such as NYO2 holistically invest in the future of orchestras:

"We have things here called play-ins where a section of the orchestra invites people of all capabilities to sign up online and download repertoires, then come for a collective jam session here at the orchestra. It's amazing to see 150 harps or 150 brass or 150 cellos—a full stage! It has been wonderful to see their hunger and passion, not only by generation, as there are 6-year-olds to amateur musicians, but also viewing the communities that participate. We are working on a very strong instrumental program here, to be able to provide instruments to our groups in Philadelphia. Engaging in such interactive ways with young people helps to build a passion and audience for music in our communities."

Partnerships with schools are crucial, despite many problems with funding and finding the right teachers, coupled with embracing all that music brings to the table beyond the pillars of English, math and science:

> "We're certainly working with school-system leaders in music education to bring the orchestra closer to students, with live music projects that we're developing, the potential for online streaming and taking music out of the concert hall. Our work with All City Orchestra, for example, gives us a way of learning the school system's working philosophy and finding new ways of engaging with them. For us, the NYO2/Carnegie Hall expansion was a wonderful opportunity to create a national connection to this conversation through Carnegie Hall's hard work and commitment, but also engaging local Philadelphians due to the responsiveness of the deep musical community here."

Conductor Gustavo Dudamel has been a vigorous and inspiring advocate for such projects. Music & artistic director of the Los Angeles Philharmonic and music director of the Simón Bolívar Symphony Orchestra of Venezuela, he has championed the Youth Orchestra Los Angeles, modeled upon Venezuela's iconic music-education program El Sistema, of which he is a graduate. YOLA exposes children in underserved communities to the wonders and joys of music, which they would otherwise have little hope of listening to or pursuing. Vulgamore and other enlightened artistic administrators are creating excitement for and building upon such proven programs, with educational and financial support that continues to grow. Her brainstorming work with Gillinson continues to yield much:

> "Clive is deeply dedicated to both great art and reach, very open to hearing new ideas and, in our case with The Philadelphia Orchestra, we've been having great fun remembering our past and letting it inform our future, most recently by expanding educational programs. He encourages a diversity of programming through Carnegie Hall that reaches far beyond New York City."

A highly engaging element of that diversity is an entire strand of curricula—Careers in Lifelong Learning—with the emphasis on supporting individuals who feel that the arts are such an important part of their lives that they continue to learn on their own well after they leave school. Part of the challenge is having that dialogue with kids at an early age. They may not end up on Broadway or at Carnegie Hall, but there are many other opportunities.

Gillinson has seen the challenge firsthand:

"Because creativity is about asking questions and making unexpected connections, it requires so much more of teachers. There are no formulae, so teachers are often learning as much as their students. There will never be too many highly motivated teachers devoted to this approach to learning. Whilst it is true that many arts organisations, schools and nonprofits work like this, there remains a vast amount to be learned about how to nurture curiosity and creativity in children."

Thinking back, Gillinson recalls:

"When I was at school, we were essentially expected to assimilate large amounts of knowledge and information. We're now living in a world where the knowledge explosion means that we will never again be able to learn everything about virtually any subject, so creativity and the ability to learn are becoming ever more important. The accelerating increase in the complexity of our world demands a very different educational model, and thus very different teachers. Many countries are now seeking to change their approach to education to address this challenge, but the ever more demanding requirements ultimately fall on the teachers; we're going to need better and better teachers who are lifelong learners themselves. Education systems in which bad teachers are protected are a tragedy and unfortunately far too common. Sadly, this problem is replicated in every area of life in which people see their jobs as being about themselves rather than those they serve—in this case, children."

During Gillinson's formative years, his unhappiness bred determination and a drive to succeed, together with endless energy. From age 8 or 9 onwards he was driven by the wish to do everything as well as he could, to explore.

"Fostering curiosity is one of the most important things that we can give to our children, combined with love, security, structure and discipline. One of the challenges of being a parent is how to help kids find what they love doing and nurture that. At the same time, they've got to learn to stick with things, to persevere. It can be very hard to find this balance, although it's absolutely vital. If they don't learn perseverance, it will almost certainly affect their ability to handle the tough times in their lives."

What can schools do to stimulate curiosity and perseverance? What happens to students who do not have creative outlets? Until much later in life, Gillinson felt that Frensham had let him down completely. It was not at all academically oriented, and they hardly pushed the students. He now realizes that this was almost certainly about the teachers, not the subjects. An area that now greatly interests him is history, yet he did not enjoy this at school. Only later did he begin to realize that, with great teaching, there is probably no subject that is not fascinating. So much of what may seem peripheral in life can wind up being crucial; he read voraciously and reading became his learning catalyst, effectively his "mentor" as it opened up a world of imagination and possibilities.

...and Teachers

The sphere of education can become compressed quite quickly, given the relentless demands that schools have as far as the criteria they must meet. Yet Gillinson makes clear that teachers must also be aware of educating the whole person rather than concentrating solely on exams: "If schools and teachers aren't assessed on the arts, they are unlikely to prioritize them, and by default the message will be that the arts don't matter. It totally depends on what is ordained from the top."

If politicians, parents or head teachers do not themselves engage with the arts, then the chances are that schools will not emphasize them either. The question of how to increase awareness and participation in the arts, particularly in light of well-established research, today remains actively pursued by large and small arts organizations alike. Teacher training is a core element of the Weill Music Institute's work, and is a key part of Carnegie Hall's mission. If it can help to develop a teacher's ability to teach music, that benefit will touch the lives of a huge number of students over the lifetime of every teacher with whom WMI works. Carnegie Hall looks for meaningful leverage in all areas of its educational work, well exemplified by the enormous benefit of sharing programs such as Link Up.

Ever since he started LSO Discovery, the LSO's education program, Gillinson has believed passionately in the educational value of the arts, thinking of such initiatives in terms of what they contribute to people's lives, not the institution:

"One fascinating and unexpected outcome of LSO Discovery was that it changed the players completely, at least those who participated, which in the early days amounted to very few! However, as the years went by, more and more players became involved, and they discovered that helping to improve other people's lives was both thrilling and fulfilling. In addition, they found that by getting involved in educational work, they were functioning as creative individuals, rarely the case when playing in a symphony orchestra. So all of a sudden, these people who were artists at heart, but who—as orchestral players—had effectively been living their lives as superb craftsmen, rediscovered the artistic piece of themselves and found that they as individuals could make a meaningful contribution. Unexpectedly, they changed and became testaments to how important it is for each individual to do something through which they can contribute to others' lives."

Lennox Mackenzie

Lennox Mackenzie, who joined the orchestra as principal first violin in 1980, then was elected to its board the year after Gillinson became managing director, marvels at LSO Discovery's expanding reach and long-lasting impact:

"By 2002, 30,000 people were being reached annually and these days over double that number per annum benefit from the programme. The American composer John Adams recently said to me that he so admires LSO Discovery, and that in his opinion it is the best orchestral-education programme in the world. Through this initiative, the LSO musicians' lives themselves were enhanced, by gaining the interest and love of music of young impressionable people, encouraging them and witnessing the moving results."

Integrating the Arts

Gillinson has constantly worked to create exposure to the arts, to sow seeds and nurture curiosity, and provide opportunities, while acknowledging that one never knows which seeds will take root and, if so, how or when. One such exploration took the LSO's bass trombonist to prison....

"When we created LSO Discovery, we asked the players if they had any particular projects they would like to propose. Our bass trombonist, Frank, said that he had long dreamed of creating a brass band in a prison. We contacted various prisons and in the end found a prison governor who liked the idea. Frank was invited down to meet the prisoners to tell them about the project in order to gauge interest. The unforgettable closing line of his introductory presentation was: 'It's very important that you all understand that it's very demanding learning to play a brass instrument, so I hope you're going to be in here for a very long time!' Undaunted, the prisoners got very involved in the project and he built a good brass band. However, as they got near to the date of their first concert, one of the prisoners was released. This became a major press story because, for the first time in British prison history, a prisoner came back to prison voluntarily, because he didn't want to miss playing in the concert: the power of music! Working in prisons is now an important and impactful part of WMI's programs."

Gillinson's colleagues are well attuned to how curiosity fosters both imagination and results. "By and large, the majority of people whom I've been lucky enough to meet, who run major institutions, are almost by definition inherently curious," observes Glenn Lowry.

"You can't be involved in these kinds of enterprises without that openness of mind and curiosity. My New York colleagues tend to be remarkable in their thirst for knowledge. This can't help but positively affect the staffs as well. People do these jobs—whether as curators, educators, conservators or administrators—because they're really interested in the place's subject. People who work at the Museum of Modern Art, for example, are deeply interested in modern and contemporary art. They want to be surrounded by the energy that comes from looking at art that's meaningful and powerful, and connecting with artists, all of which are highly motivating."

The other side of that dynamic scenario, however, is generally more prevalent. "Sadly, the vast majority of people end up in jobs that are not stimulating," Gillinson observes.

"They're simply earning a living rather than living a vocation. If people can spend their lives doing something they're passionate about, they're much more likely to retain their curiosity and continue to grow. People doing work that is utterly routine are understandably likely to shut off to a greater or lesser extent. Yet some, even in jobs that are relatively boring, have got something inside them that seeks to find more, always trying to do better, to innovate, to improve. It's so important that we try to help people find the areas in which they can get creatively involved on a personal level, especially if this is not a dimension offered to them in their working lives."

Michael Tilson Thomas shares his perspective on this crucial challenge:

"Since I go back with Clive such a long way, I see all of the things he does in perhaps a more direct, humanistic way. They're part and parcel of who he is and always has been. The things he's learned over the years, as we all have, make what we do and love more possible. What we're really all involved with doing is trying to wrestle dreams into reality. As with any large organization, there are just so many details to be addressed with times, schedules, rules, lists... trying to get the dream to survive all of those things and still keep its spontaneity and revelation is an ongoing challenge."

Those dreams, though, often do not have any chance of becoming reality. Joseph Polisi has seen first-hand how the No Child Left Behind law, and the extensive testing that accompanied it, has long-term harmed the creativity of K-12 classrooms throughout the United States. One of his goals at the Wallace Foundation, where he is a board member, is to look at knowledge gaps. They also study artistic and aesthetic education, and its value within the larger context of K-12 education.

"The key question is how to integrate this kind of education on a daily basis so that children directly benefit from such experience. Testing tells only one side of the child, and schools—especially elementary and middle—that have a robust artistic atmosphere invariably tend to have a safer, less combative or frightening environment, better teacher opportunities and more active ways for parents to become involved."

In speaking with principals in the New York school system, Polisi found them to be judged on math, science and reading test results, but at the same time concerned that there is no metric whatsoever and no positive reinforcement if they succeed on the arts side:

"If they have a vibrant arts program, it does not show up on the screen, which has to be changed. That, though, is a very long process. I'm a product of the New York City school system from grades 1 through 12—in my day in the '50s and '60s it was an incredibly robust arts environment with thousands of children given instruments to play and taught by competent music teachers. But the infrastructure fell hard in the '70s and never really came back. Sadly, we're now reaping what we've sown. Why do we expect parents, administrators and teachers who've had essentially no arts education between K-12, and into universities for that matter, to now embrace aesthetic education and the arts? To them it's like going after Boolean algebra! It's so far afield that they're not sure what it is."

They are also suspicious. The arts have been pummeled by national and local politicians since the Mapplethorpe controversy of the late 1980s. "What politician on the federal, state or local level is a true advocate of the arts today?" Polisi asks.

> "Very few, because there's no political capital in it. The arts as an entity have gone away from the psyche of American educators, politicians and leaders. It's difficult because the infrastructure no longer exists as it once did, and the arts are sometimes considered to be a waste of time in the context of the math, science and reading curricula—all of these prejudices. The arts-education establishment has not done a very good job of making the case; we're in a real fix."

Espousing the Journey

There are extraordinary accomplishments like Ensemble Connect, and in many ways arts education in the United States is the leader in the world, in terms of curriculum, facilities, faculty and performances, yet the country is not generally supporting the arts. "The reason that I'm genuinely optimistic, though, is that I'm very spoiled," Polisi acknowledges.

> "I'm surrounded by about 825 idealists who are young dancers, actors and musicians. I see their idealism, their dedication, their artistry every single day, and I say to myself thank God, because they're just not going to be put down. Something's going to happen, and it does! You see all the innovation that's happening, whether it's 'Hamilton' on Broadway, new choreography and plays, new music... they're out there creating. But wouldn't it be wonderful if they could actually be supported as well?"

Supporting and serving people through music and education were among Leonard Bernstein's great loves and gifts. Gillinson recalls a dinner he had with conductor and pianist Daniel Barenboim, when their conversation turned to Bernstein:

> "Daniel told me a story that demonstrated why he revered Leonard Bernstein so much. One evening at dinner with him, the conversation turned to Bruckner's Symphony No. 8, which Daniel was conducting at that time. In response to his passionate advocacy

of it, Bernstein said that he didn't think it was a very good piece and when Daniel asked why, Bernstein went over to the piano and played through the entire first movement by heart, pointing out all the things about which he had reservations. Daniel couldn't believe that anyone would have studied a piece in such depth without even wishing to conduct it. He found it awe-inspiring."

Bernstein, of course, was an extraordinary polymath, yet something like this could never have happened unless he was a passionate explorer of all music, which came through not only in all of his music-making, but in everything he did.

One of the purposes of Carnegie Hall's festivals-cross-disciplinary cultural collaborations with other institutions, centered around a theme, that Carnegie Hall launched in New York in 2007—is to encourage audiences to explore outside their comfort zone and experience very different sorts of events. They may respond passionately or not, but the exploration itself can be fascinating and opens up so many perspectives, akin to trying Japanese fugu or Uruguayan choripán for the first time. "One of the concerts in our 'Berlin in Lights' festival involved a pretty way-out contemporary ensemble from Berlin," Gillinson recalls.

"At intermission I saw one of our trustees, Mercedes Bass, heading for the exit. I was thrilled that she had attended, as she normally goes only to classical music concerts, so I went over to ask if she'd enjoyed the evening. Her answer was, 'Clive, do you know the saying "curiosity killed the cat"? Well, this cat is dead!' However, what mattered was that the festival had tempted her to explore new possibilities."

Jessye Norman gratefully recognizes this trait:

"Carnegie Hall is sold out for an evening of Beethoven and an evening of gospel choirs! Clive devotes equal know-how to making certain that it all succeeds, that the word is spread, that those who have never thought of attending a performance at Carnegie Hall find themselves sitting in one of the most glorious music centers ever... waiting to bathe in one of the purest and most luscious natural acoustics in the world."

4
Questioning Accepted Wisdom

People often think that adhering to the status quo enables them to avoid risk, offering a safe way forward when faced with challenging situations. The celebrated economist, author, Harvard professor and diplomat, John Kenneth Galbraith, observed:

> "The shortcomings of economics are not original error but uncorrected obsolescence. The obsolescence has occurred because what is convenient has become sacrosanct. Anyone who attacks such ideas must seem to be a trifle self-confident and even aggressive. The man who makes his entry by leaning against an infirm door gets an unjustified reputation for violence. Something is to be attributed to the poor state of the door."

The challenge is that human nature seeks certainties rather than embracing uncertainty. When Gillinson began at Carnegie Hall and started engaging the senior staff around major questions, he found a degree of reluctance among some of them to challenge the way things had been done in the past. It is easier to live with established answers than open questions, as these can result in not being able to resolve a situation right away, a more challenging—and often more liberating—environment in which to work. Engaging the minds of a top team will almost always ensure better answers than having a leader alone make the decisions, even though there are clearly times when a leader has to lead. As with any democracy, involving and empowering people is much harder to control; yet control, as Gillinson reflects, is not the important thing.

> "Democracy demonstrates many weaknesses, frequently due to poor leadership. Those who don't have a clear vision, but whose primary objective is to seek (and stay in) power, carry a huge responsibility for weakening government. One need look no further than Congress

in recent times. Many people who genuinely care about the US, and know how important it is for the world that America should be strong and successful, speak about how Congress demonstrates the intrinsic weakness of Western, or more particularly, US democracy. To see the country's leaders threatening chaos, and occasionally making the US appear ungovernable, is almost incomprehensible to outside friends; this is not just bad for the US but for the world. Democracy has huge weaknesses as well as strengths, but it does depend on strong and visionary leadership. As Winston Churchill pithily said: 'No one pretends that democracy is perfect or all wise. It may be a bad system of government, but all the others are worse!'"

People fear the unknown, which is why they prefer answers, even if those answers are not good. So often, when young adults come to Gillinson and others in his position for career advice, they want definitive answers: If you do this, then that will happen. This can be extremely poor advice. "Career paths—and, in fact, life—cannot be controlled like that, which is why I always ask them what they're passionate about, and suggest they allow that to be their guide, giving it everything they've got whilst keeping a completely open mind. Then their talent and passion will lead them." The outcome of this journey is rarely possible to predict; trying to define and follow preplanned paths will likely result in great opportunities passing unnoticed, both for people and organizations. Gillinson completely understands that this sort of advice can be quite tough for young people in search of answers.

> "It's a natural thing to be scared of uncertainty, yet liberating to know that it's perfectly alright to feel that way. When I was younger I wanted the same thing—certainty—and it took me a long time to realise that uncertainty can be a strength rather than weakness, because uncertainty also brings with it endless possibilities."

Control

In today's society, people are much more open to portfolio-type careers, rather than simply following a straight or prescribed path. In addition, those in their 20s and 30s are much less rigid in their thinking about jobs, more open to exploring and considering what they love, what they can put back into society.

It is likewise fascinating to consider how the relationship between orchestral musicians and conductors has changed over the years. At one time, the accepted wisdom was that conductors needed to tyrannize orchestras in order to gain and maintain respect. For example, to underline his power, George Szell would sometimes ask players to play the most difficult parts of a concert one player at a time, in front of all their colleagues, to enable him to hear how every one of them played it—a terrifying ordeal for even the best orchestral player. Many other great conductors of that era, such as Arturo Toscanini, Fritz Reiner and Herbert von Karajan, performed extraordinary concerts, but frequently at the expense of terrified musicians. By the time Gillinson started playing in the LSO in 1970, the conductor/player relationship had changed and was, in many cases, more like a battle for supremacy, with many orchestral players exchanging heated words with the conductor.

Gillinson recalls one of the most memorable of such moments at the LSO:

"We were in a recording session and the conductor, Nello Santi, was asking something of the principal trumpet, who was also the LSO's player-chairman. Try as Santi would, he could not get him to play the passage of music as asked. In the end, in exasperation, the player-chairman said, 'If you knew anything at all about trumpet playing, you would know that what you are asking of me is impossible.' Santi quietly put down his conductor's baton, walked gently round the orchestra, picked up the trumpet and played it exactly as he had been asking for. I guess he'd been waiting all his life for that moment; in his entire career I doubt that he ever received more applause than he did then—certainly never more laughter!"

Over the last few decades, the conductor/orchestra model has largely moved to one that mirrors today's more enlightened management practices; players and conductors now tend toward being partners in making great music. Although this is in many ways a more challenging model for conductors, as they have to earn the respect of the players through every aspect of their artistry and craft, it is also far more satisfying and inspirational for all involved.

Gillinson has concerns about US orchestras' music-director model, in that it encompasses a fundamental conflict of interest:

"Most conductor/music-directors have the power to decide who their orchestra engages as guest conductors, and not enough have the confidence to want to be surrounded by the very best. In addition, music directors usually have control over the repertoire that they and every guest conductor performs, and they are not always the best judges of what they themselves perform best, let alone being able to acknowledge that there is another conductor who might perform some music better than they do. With an artistic director working for the administrative team, whose only job is to ensure that the greatest possible conductors and soloists are engaged, and the finest concerts planned, these conflicts of interest are eliminated. It is vital for all organisational models to ensure that those making decisions never have their own self-interest at stake."

Another Way

Those receptive to challenge, to questioning—and make no mistake, many "powerful" people welcome this dialogue—do not take it as criticism, but as a means of looking at how things can be done better. Jonathan Vaughan notes that "challenging accepted wisdom tends to come with the territory of constantly asking questions and being curious. In Clive's case, it's not a process of iconoclasm for the sake of it, but more about a position of trying to understand things in great detail."

Ian Martin recalls that among Gillinson's favorite expressions is "Let's look at this from another side." When coming up against brick walls, which should be added to death and taxes as a trilogy of the inevitable, one must determine how to get around them. Martin readily acknowledges things that they should have done differently.

> "Lightness on one's feet is key; if plans need to be changed, then people should not hesitate to proceed in a different way. LSO St. Luke's opened in 2003, nine years after we first began to talk about it. It required tremendous tenacity: five years in the planning and four years in delivery. The hall is doing brilliantly now, part of London's artistic and education scene, fully utilised almost 365 days a year—morning, afternoon and evening."

The word "insurmountable" could well have been coined for LSO St. Luke's, not only for the once-derelict and withering building itself, but for the unlikelihood of what it would become. Why are some people hardwired to take on such projects and, for others, navigating Manhattan traffic is challenge enough? "Clive is one of those people naturally predisposed to rail against the status quo," Glenn Lowry notes.

"He's always thinking about what the next move could be and doesn't worry too much about what established wisdom says. At the same time, while thoughtful and measured in his decision-making, he's interested in moving the mark. People like that don't spend a whole lot of time worrying about the status quo. But in complex jobs like his, one has to be fully aware of the status quo; one can move the dial only at a certain time. If at the wrong moment it'll go nowhere. He's an extremely strategic thinker."

So many professionals struggle with the necessity to be open-minded: Think of a heart surgeon used to traditional bypass surgery on a heart-lung machine who adheres to his original training, rather than embracing—when applicable— minimally invasive cardiac surgery through a smaller incision, or new techniques that permit replacement of a heart valve through a catheter in the leg, with no chest incision whatsoever. Then translate that to every single profession in which progress is measured by meaningful change. There is a reason that Apple Computer and Google are the world's most valuable companies, and while Carnegie Hall may not similarly flirt with a trillion-dollar valuation, there is a reason that it continues among the world's most influential and far-reaching cultural and educational institutions.

On the education front, Gillinson repeatedly stresses the need for people to find what they love, whatever the accepted wisdom would have them believe, then foster a way to put that into play to contribute to others' lives. This mindset directly helps young people to think beyond themselves. Unfortunately, at many of the schools where the Carnegie Hall team works, countless students have neither backup skills nor adequate support from their parents.

Finding What Works

During the 21 years that Gillinson managed the LSO, he and his team undertook fascinating and transformational new projects, in many ways redefining the nature of a symphony orchestra. Against the odds, these included creating the first-of-its-kind LSO Live—the orchestra's own record label—and transforming that derelict old church near the Barbican into LSO St. Luke's.

Gillinson's overarching passion is to do what he believes in, while at the same time encouraging individuality and making clear that his way may well not work or be relevant for others. "We never suggest that anyone should copy us, nor do we proselytise or tell other organisations what to do or how to do anything. However, we are always open to sharing our resources if asked to do so." Similarly, he is very clear about Carnegie Hall's values, but, when asked for these by anyone seeking to define their own organization's values, responds that they must define their own.

Like his mother, Gillinson is an enduring optimist, a central part of his temperament and character. Many people get bogged down by problems, having to conform to norms and being scared of change, but he sees opportunities.

"It's not to my credit; it's in the genes. As a result, almost everything is exciting and interesting to me, because any given problem or circumstance almost always offers possibilities, even if it is only the problem that is visible at first sight. One thing I always look for in the people with whom I want to work is positivity. I cannot work with those who look at a challenge or problem and say why not. I need to be inspired by those who ask how."

Lennox Mackenzie reflects:

"Clive's leadership defined the LSO as the 20th century drew to a close. For us as musicians, to witness this was astonishing. We knew Clive as a friendly section cellist who had a hobby of running an antique shop in upmarket Hampstead. He played football [soccer] with the LSO team and was always joking. He accepted a task that he himself was unsure of being able to accomplish, something he admitted at the time. He was forever probing new concepts and ideas while genuinely listening to the orchestra's members, at the same time persuading our funders through well-thought-out concepts to donate significantly larger grants to create a bigger orchestra and ensure a better lifestyle for our members. Touring, for example, has always been an important facet of the orchestra's work. He appointed a Japanese businessman, Hiroaki Yamataka, as the LSO's International vice president and Yamasan (as he was known) brought the interest and sponsorship of many Japanese companies, allowing us to be able to tour the Far East. Clive also put in place a residency with New York's Lincoln Center, meaning that the LSO appeared annually in New York and the USA, which it does to this day."

These actions—including changing the governance of the orchestra to bring in expertise from key business fields—created a desirable situation in which the European Union's very best players were attracted to the LSO, a stark contrast to the accepted wisdom of just a few years earlier, when few would have predicted their being universally recognized as the top UK orchestra and one of the greatest in the world.

Questioning accepted wisdom is, of course, only the first step, as difficult as that may be to take. Mackenzie recalls the LSO's dismal days:

> "When Clive accepted the position of managing director, he was tasked initially with two vital assignments: bringing the orchestra's accounts back into the black and solving the lack of audiences in its new home, the Barbican. The orchestra had a deficit of approximately £350,000, a huge sum to the LSO in those days. Orchestras in the UK are reliant on funding from the Arts Council, a government agency that distributes public money to arts organizations. The agreement in our contract to play at the Barbican means that the City of London also funds the LSO. At that time, the relationship the LSO had with our funders was at an all-time low. Historically there has always been the question as to whether there are too many orchestras in London and when one of them is seen to be incapable of managing its books, questions are asked and press speculation occurs."

The Arts Council gave Gillinson and the board three years to eliminate the deficit. The orchestra was hemorrhaging money because of the nature of the contract that had been agreed with the City to play at the Barbican. Four one-month subscription series were the order of the day, an imported US model with no relevance to the London music scene, and audiences were not attending. The repertoire was also seen as too ambitious and modernistic. Mackenzie continues:

> "It was important to ensure that through this difficult time the players' earnings were maintained and Clive tasked his administration to find as much commercial work as possible for the players, which also brought in much-needed management fees for the LSO itself. To save money, there were fewer concert rehearsals at this time and standards were compromised, a fact that worried and frustrated Clive and the rest of us enormously. He could not wait to eliminate the deficit and look to the future. He learned fast, though, and within two years the orchestra was in the black again, a year earlier than the deadline imposed on him by the Arts Council—a champagne moment! One could make an analogy with what was happening in the UK during that time: After crazy spending over many years that

brought us massive debts, the need for a period of austerity, hard work and careful use of public money took hold."

For much of his LSO career, Gillinson became ever more frustrated with the fact that, despite their words of admiration for the LSO, the Arts Council did not typically reward excellence, but annually took the easy option of giving broadly the same funding to all of the orchestras. As Mackenzie observed:

"Clive wanted the LSO to be the flag bearer for British orchestras and I believe that has been achieved. I am also aware that the hard work and innovation and endless probing for new ideas must continue if the LSO is to retain that position. I learned from him never to sit on my hands but to constantly look for ideas that excite and stimulate."

One such idea took shape at the end of the first Gulf War in February 1991. An Israeli promoter wrote to every major orchestra in the world to ask if they would be willing to come to Israel in the middle of April—an absurdly short two months away—to help start cultural life again. During the Gulf War, Saddam Hussein had been trying to draw Israel into the war by firing scud missiles at the country, and cultural life had ground to a halt. Every orchestra that responded, and most did not, said that it was completely impossible to arrange such a project at two months' notice. Gillinson, though, discussed it with the board and got their agreement to try to make it happen if at all possible. He and his team began working on it immediately, first figuring out how to rearrange the orchestra's schedule and then how to raise the money. This had to be completed by mid-March to secure their El Al flights. In addition, since they assumed that some players would be worried about going, they wanted to talk to the orchestra and give every player the right not to go. To help the players decide, Gillinson brought in an expert from the Foreign Office to give a briefing and answer questions. In the end, very few players decided not to go and, after a gargantuan effort, they raised all of the requisite funds with little more than an hour to spare.

As well as donations, they had some wonderful responses. For example, they approached Ted Arison of Carnival Cruise Lines about making a donation, but he declined, saying that all of his charitable work in Israel supported Israeli organizations. He did, however, offer to buy 2,000 tickets across all of the LSO's Israel concerts to give away to recent Jewish immigrants from Russia, who could not afford to buy them. The extraordinary emotion and success of the tour became an indelibly positive sign of the orchestra's flexibility and drive, with Israeli audiences expressing heartfelt appreciation for everything that the LSO had done to make it possible.

5

Creating a Magnet for Talent

Given its history, name recognition and stature, Carnegie Hall is in a position to attract top players—on both sides of the stage—across all disciplines and in every area of its work. Gillinson believes that every aspect of what he and the team do, and the way they design each program, has to ensure that the hall attracts and retains the finest performers, trustees, staff, supporters and, ultimately, audiences—creating an irresistible magnet for the best talent across the entire organization. This mindset pervades everything that the Hall undertakes. In addition, each aspect of the organization is interrelated in creating irresistible magnets for talent: trustees, staff, the artistic and educational mission, the philosophy itself. Everything that Carnegie Hall does supports, reinforces and enhances every other aspect.

Carnegie Hall's creation of the National Youth Orchestra of the USA (NYO-USA) is a prime example of this philosophy. The only way such a project could achieve the highest aspirations would be if it attracted the very finest 16- to 19-year-old musicians from across the nation. To do this, every aspect of the experience had to be unmissable. Thus Carnegie Hall engaged one of the world's greatest conductors for the inaugural tour, Valery Gergiev; recruited the very finest principal players from the top US orchestras to coach the young musicians; arranged concerts at the Kennedy Center in Washington, the top halls in Moscow and St. Petersburg, and at the Proms in London; and negotiated national television broadcasts of the Moscow and London concerts... all of this before a single player had been chosen. By creating this virtuous circle from inception, every dimension enabled the NYO-USA to start at the pinnacle of quality, an almost impossible achievement without the leverage of the Carnegie Hall brand and reputation.

This is the lens through which Carnegie Hall looks when developing all of its major projects: the massive renovation project in 1986, development of the artist-curated *Perspectives* series, the creation of Zankel Hall and the Weill Music Institute in 2003, the national and international festivals, Ensemble Connect,

NYO-USA, NYO2, the creation of the Resnick Education Wing, the national rollout of Link Up, and many more.

Given the choice, most employees couple the need to make a living with enjoyment of their job and the desire to make a difference. What are their passions? What gets them up in the morning beyond the weekly payroll? And once on board, are they given the freedom to excel, to advance their careers, to be creative, to enjoy their work, to make a genuine contribution to the organization and its mission?

The aura of Carnegie Hall's name, burnished to a singular luster over the 125 years since it opened in 1891, can only take its staff so far. They are the ones who walk, take the subway and hail cabs to get to work day in and day out, so unless the leadership is both supportive and receptive, that same walk, subway or cab ride can just as easily move away from West 57th Street. Current and potential employees are drawn to a compelling mission, a collaborative and exciting work environment, and leadership that engenders trust and offers true role models. A good salary helps, yet is consistently in third or fourth place in study after study that traces job satisfaction. Offering room to grow, to make a creative contribution and the opportunity to advance are strong motivators, yet even they are rarely enough without a clear and inspiring mission. Given the kaleidoscopic range of upbringings, experience, intelligence, motivation and capacity among people around the world, the values to which they—indeed most of us—generally respond are remarkably similar.

At Carnegie Hall and similarly enlightened organizations—whether small and local or huge and international—those values rarely differ, which is another exciting lure for creative young people. They are eager to hang out after hours, to enjoy fellowship, brainstorming and problem-solving, to make a difference both within and beyond their immediate sphere, to move past rigid templates.

Management's accessibility and openness to share are further magnets within an environment that may well have its share of uncertainty, whether from the economy or public response. Are employees free—nay encouraged— to question the status quo, to offer alternatives, to speak up? Do both new and longtime employees feel the personal and professional investment from those who sign their paychecks, while fostering loyalty well beyond the numbers? Is communication transparent? The motivation of any organization's leadership cannot be faked. To be sure, this press release or that internal document may point to skills, results, purpose and goals, yet over time the real arc of direction presses through the surface and eventually becomes indelibly clear to the point that it can be inherently trusted.

Cities also recognize the need to support a vibrant cultural and creative life, which then encourages everything from real estate to restaurants: the definition of symbiotic relationships and societal cohesion. Within this environment, ticket sales are rarely far behind.

Standards and Morale

London has always understood the importance of the LSO to its cultural life, as have the orchestra's musicians. When Gillinson came on board, he was determined to improve their lot concurrent with the position and health of the orchestra itself, realizing that to improve playing standards, players had to work less, thereby creating more time for relaxation and home practice, and the development of other outlets for their creativity. However, that meant they needed to be paid more for each appearance. Also, Gillinson wished to attract not only top UK players to the orchestra, but also the finest international players. Finally, he felt deeply that the musicians needed a fixed holiday period. The orchestra's Lennox Mackenzie recalls with wonder "how hard it was to believe that we didn't have a fixed holiday before this mini revolution!"

It meant creating new systems within the orchestra and finding more money. The standard of living for UK musicians in those days, compared with much of the rest of the world, was low and Gillinson knew this. Morale was poor.

"Conductors were often amazed at the work schedules we achieved," Mackenzie marvels.

> "The great Dutch maestro Bernard Haitink used to say to me, 'I really don't know how UK musicians cope with their schedule. But I admire them so much for doing so!' The LSO board agreed that Clive should take his ideas to the funders for consideration. He presented his paper to the Arts Council in an ambitious attempt to obtain what was advertised at that time as 'Enhancement Funding' from the Council. His visionary ideas impressed the body hugely and they ultimately awarded the extra monies to the LSO to put into place these new systems and life-changing ideas."

Gillinson went on to persuade the Corporation of the City of London—owners of the Barbican, Europe's largest arts center and the LSO's home—to match the Arts Council's enhanced funding. The difference this made to members' lives was incalculable. It also created the situation in which the LSO could seriously aim to become one of the world's leading orchestras. Mackenzie continues:

> "It is worth stressing that whilst all these improvements were occurring, the ethos and underlying spirit of the LSO as a self-governing orchestra, where the players are shareholders of the company and party to all decisions made through its elected board, was maintained. Clive—having been a member-player—was fully supportive and believed in this ongoing governance. He was also concerned about the legacy that the LSO left to future generations, and instigated many commissions from UK and overseas composers, with world premieres given by the orchestra. Exploring new music always generates challenges to audiences, but by then trust had been created and interest in new music grew. Clive ensured an acceptable equilibrium to programmes so they still appealed to what was by then our core audience."

Another issue of great concern to Gillinson was the decline in recordings of classical music. The huge historical selection of core-repertoire recordings available on store shelves had resulted in the major recording companies reducing their new classical-music projects to a bare minimum. Gillinson felt that the LSO—both for reasons of legacy and for its ongoing worldwide profile and reputation—needed to be recording the repertoire that defined its current artistic identity with the conductors on whom this identity and reputation were being built. "Thus Clive hatched the idea of LSO Live," Mackenzie reminisces.

> "After much discussion and deliberation, and many orchestra and union meetings, a contract was drawn up whereby players and conductors did not receive any fees for the recordings made live from concerts, but participated in a profit-sharing plan. CDs were priced at a low level, therefore allowing everyone to listen to our music at home and whilst travelling, which continues to this day. Without such an agreement, the world would have missed out on what I term as Sir Colin Davis's Indian summer, during which he recorded an astonishing amount of music, including major pieces of Berlioz, Elgar, Sibelius, Nielsen, Dvořák, Smetana and Verdi, to mention but a few. Grammys were won, amongst many other awards. Some recording companies responded to the competition by initially dropping the LSO from their recordings, but as time passed,

the arrangement came to be copied by many of the world's leading orchestras and is now regarded as an acceptable norm. No wonder we refer to it as LSO Clive!"

When Gillinson took over as interim manager of the LSO, he discovered that Davis had decided not to continue as its principal guest conductor and had accepted several dates with London's Philharmonia Orchestra.

"We all thought he was a wonderful conductor, although incredibly sensitive to any slight; he found the LSO's culture too aggressive and cynical. His sensitivity was illustrated in a story he told me at my first meeting with him. Arriving for an LSO rehearsal, he was greeted by the principal flautist who said jokingly, 'Not you again!' Davis was convinced that he meant it, no matter how much the flautist insisted that he was joking. Nonetheless, we all wanted Sir Colin to stay, so I went to meet with him in his home, to try to persuade him to change his mind. I took him through all our planned changes, including transforming the LSO's culture to one where the music always came first. We had a very long conversation but at the end he said wistfully, 'Clive, I love what you're saying, but idealists never win.' However, being a fair man, he promised to drop the Philharmonia dates and give us a chance. As the transformation of the LSO culture progressed, Sir Colin got more and more involved until we all agreed that he should be our next principal conductor when Michael Tilson Thomas retired from the post. When I met with Sir Colin to offer him the position, which he enthusiastically accepted, I couldn't resist reminding him of what he had said all those years before, that idealists never win. As we concluded our agreement, I was delighted to be able to say: 'It's only idealists who win.'"

Sir Colin went on to become the longest-serving principal conductor in the orchestra's history, and acknowledged this era as the most important and enjoyable of his musical life.

Compelling Environment

Gillinson makes clear that every organization has to define a compelling vision based on who it serves, what their needs are and what it can contribute to their lives:

"There should be a meaningful and definable need for every organisation's existence. Our job today is to define how Carnegie Hall, uniquely, can serve people through music. Most importantly, it is about the institution serving people, not about people serving the institution. As Isaac Stern once said, 'New Yorkers have an edifice complex', so we should beware! Too often managers and boards get absorbed with the glory, brand or success of the institution. These are only achieved if the institution serves people in a meaningful and inspirational way. In smaller communities, where the constituency can often be more singular and is largely local, arts organizations will only succeed if they are utterly relevant to their community. The answers they come up with will, and should be, completely different from the answers that, for example, Carnegie Hall determines; it has to serve New York City, of course, but in common with other major national and international organisations, it also has to serve a multiplicity of other constituencies. What remains vital is that every organisation develop a unique vision that is relevant for its own environment, which always requires individual answers; there are no formulae."

At both the LSO and Carnegie Hall, Gillinson has always sought to give people the opportunity to contribute as individuals:

"Our senior staff has a lot of autonomy and space, as I believe in delegation and empowerment. I also encourage this approach throughout the organisation. My current senior team is wonderful in this way. If we wish to appoint and keep good people, we've got to empower and inspire them, and all of us share this belief."

As an LSO player and for a number of years the orchestra's chairman, Jonathan Vaughan observes that Gillinson has always sought to work with the very best people available in all areas of the organization. Combining this with aspiring to and, in fact, achieving excellence in all activities, people are naturally drawn to these environments where smaller successes open up into successively more compelling accomplishments.

"For example, when we started LSO Live, there were a number of artists who didn't want to sign up for it because they or their manager thought they should receive a fee. Rather than panicking and trying to sign those who didn't want to, Clive set about developing a label that showcased the finest artists, using the best producers and engineers in the business to produce a really high-quality product. By the following year people were falling over themselves to appear on the label."

Fostering a stimulating environment for talent remains essential. Emanuel Ax has seen firsthand that Gillinson's coworkers seem very happy.

"This is an incredible talent, because he's got to work with so many people and has to take into account their own creative personalities, their own talents. How that meshes is key—getting everyone not to obey but rather to work toward the same aim. It's like a great conductor, someone who doesn't necessarily impose his will on an orchestra, but makes its players feel that they'd genuinely like to do it that way. It's got to center on collaboration. Musicians shouldn't make music because they're scared but because they want to do it in a certain way. I think of conductors like Yannick Nézet-Séguin; what an extraordinary person, with whom to make music is unforgettable, and the orchestra *loves* him."

To make music, to present music, to provide music education, to work together for the larger good… strong magnets indeed.

6

Pursuing Must-Exist Projects

Innumerable considerations come into play when developing any new project: establishing a compelling vision, assessing the positives and negatives about the environment in which it may have to compete, weighing the risks, considering whether the organization is the right one to be undertaking it, and ensuring the creation of a clear business model and implementation plan that will maximize the chances of its success. Gillinson and his team have become quite adept at these models. Within this framework, his number-one starting point is always to be thrilled with the idea.

> "Can the world live without it? With the National Youth Orchestra of the USA, we started with an aspiration that totally captivated us. We then had to define a compelling mission and test the concept rigorously. Does it have to exist? Can we create a magnet for the finest talent? Can we build the right structure to manage and support the project? Have we fully assessed the risks and how best to protect ourselves against them? After all of these were clear, we then had to create a sound business plan. Organisations must have both an utterly compelling vision and the ability to deliver that vision, because without the requisite skills and expertise to deliver, even the best ideas will likely fail."

Ironically, Gillinson has never actually been involved in any formal management training, which he considers his loss, yet in some ways this "lack" enables the kind of open and flexible mind that has repeatedly proven to be an asset. Many potential employees come to seek a job at Carnegie Hall with extensive management training and sparkling résumés, yet very often they think in boxes, feeling that they have learned all the answers. The best training teaches the skill to ask necessary and probing questions without preconceptions. Too much of the wrong sort of training can in fact knock creativity right off the stage.

Mstislav Rostropovich & Gillinson

Gillinson fondly recalls his first meeting with the legendary cellist Mstislav Rostropovich—they would come to develop a very close personal and professional relationship spanning many years—that represents a testament to both the work ethic and how some must-exist projects gestate:

"After Slava Rostropovich had agreed to bring his 60th-birthday series to the LSO, I arranged to meet with him to discuss his program ideas. I had never met him before and he had been such a legend throughout my adult life that I somehow assumed he must be dead! He suggested that I fly to the United States and come to Carnegie Hall, where he was doing a major concert with the National Symphony Orchestra, playing a concerto in the first half and conducting a symphony in the second. He said we could talk after the concert, so once the applause had finally died down, I rushed backstage and from about 10 to 11 p.m. he greeted and endlessly kissed friends and admirers, then at about 11:15 said to me, 'Now we talk.' I asked if he was too tired and might prefer to meet the following morning, but he made it very clear that there was no problem about meeting right away. We talked until about 12:30 a.m. and planned the entire festival, which to me had become an absolutely unmissable project. When we had finished, I asked if he would like me to carry his cello back to his hotel and he said, 'No, no... now I practice.' I left Carnegie Hall to the strains of him practicing the cello, probably the only person (apart from the security guard) left in the building. The next day he had another concert—what a first impression!"

Queen Elizabeth The Queen Mother,
Rostropovich & Gillinson

St. Luke's

So many projects begin in unexpected ways, yet the word "coincidence" in describing some circumstances can seem far too tame. At the very start of the LSO Music Education Centre's development, Gillinson describes a spectacular piece of luck. He had arranged a regular catch-up meeting with Lisa Spiro, a member of the LSO Advisory Council, who managed the social-responsibility strategy for UBS, one of the world's leading banks. They sat down to talk and he asked how everything was going at UBS; she said they had just put the finishing touches to their new community-engagement plans. He asked what they were and she described a project that would involve restoring an at-risk historic building and engaging—through education—with communities in the area of that building. Hardly able to believe what he had just heard, he casually responded:

> "'You're not going to believe this, Lisa, but this morning we sent off a feasibility-study proposal for your project!' I described our St. Luke's Music Education project to her: that St. Luke's was a derelict,

at-risk, Hawksmoor church in an area of great social need near the Barbican. She asked what we were looking for and I told her that we thought we would be seeking a lead (named) sponsor for 25% of the cost. She said that she would discuss our project with UBS's leadership once we had the first cost estimate. We continued with the feasibility study, surveys and a range of other detailed work, and the estimated cost came in at £14 million (just over $20 million). The day arrived when she had arranged for the top brass from UBS, including one of their most senior people from Switzerland, to visit the site for a tour. The church consisted of no more than four crumbling walls and a spire, and the grounds had long been considered too dangerous for public access. Because of this, the local council had kept the property bolted for many years. We had the key to the padlock, as we needed regular access for the investigative work we were doing. However, just before the UBS team rolled up in their sparkling BMWs, we suddenly discovered that our key didn't work, as the council must have changed the locks since our last visit. We kept the UBS people talking whilst one of our team ran off to try to find a workman nearby with a hacksaw. By great luck we found one, and he mysteriously agreed to lend it to us (I guess our story was so absurd that he believed it); we cut through the chains, went in and showed the UBS team around the church and site. We loved the fact that the first act of bringing our lead sponsor into St. Luke's was achieved through breaking and entering, albeit legally."

Now among the world's most vibrant and iconic music-education centers, the birth of LSO St. Luke's consisted of a labor of trials. As part of the project, they had to dismantle the ceiling of the crypt, which was the church's ground-level floor. The area was overgrown with high grass, much of it head height, and all of them had been walking on it as they developed the concept for the project and showed the architect, builders and potential funders around. However, as soon as the construction company started removing the floor, which was scheduled to take a number of days, the entire floor collapsed. Had that happened earlier, the overgrown grass may well have continued to grow for a very long time. Needless to say, the demolition of the floor was the only part of the project that was completed ahead of schedule!

Reputation and Trust

As the LSO began to right itself and glimpse its long-obscured light, the next steps could begin. "Now that we were back on course, it was clearly the time to start rehearsing for proper periods of time," Lennox Mackenzie remembers.

> "Clive was determined to improve the orchestra's reputation and to do that perceptions needed to be changed. He felt that members needed to set aside the pursuit of short-term personal gain and concentrate on making great music and building esteem with every performance. He was certain that if we could achieve that, all the benefits would flow naturally. To do this the orchestra needed the finest conductors and musicians with whom to work, and audiences would attend in droves—spend money to make money."

Gillinson organized thematic festivals with the greatest conductors of the day, including Leonard Bernstein, Michael Tilson Thomas, Sir Colin Davis, Mstislav Rostropovich, Sir Georg Solti and Pierre Boulez; the resulting trust and belief engendered by these programs brought large audiences to the Barbican. He enjoyed close and meaningful relationships with all of these artists—as a manager, to be sure, yet crucially also as a fellow musician—that resulted in their keenness to become involved in the LSO's future. He had gained their trust and they in turn admired his visionary outlook, eagerly participating in what "must exist." Mackenzie smiles when describing one of countless good times that went well beyond the business at hand: "A prime example of this was the great cellist Rostropovich turning up to one of Clive's birthday parties unexpectedly, dressed in a gorilla outfit. There followed much hugging!"

Gillinson warmly remembers the event:

> "Whilst I was managing the LSO, the orchestra put on a surprise birthday party for me. When I came into the room I was greeted by players and the administration, as well as my whole family. After the party had been in full swing for a while, the door burst open and in bounded a gorilla, which leapt around the room, swung from the door, grabbed the birthday cake, laid it down on the floor and started gobbling it—a remarkably badly behaved gorilla. After a few minutes of gorilla bedlam, somebody came into the room and said, 'Clive, to remind you of your previous life as a cellist,' and handed a cello to the gorilla, which took it but had no idea how to play it, holding the

bow in the wrong hand and in every way making a complete hash of it. Someone then suggested that I show the gorilla how to hold the cello and bow, so slightly patronizingly I tried to show it what to do. Suddenly the gorilla got the hang of it and played 'Happy Birthday' superbly—it was Slava Rostropovich. I understand that when the administrative team asked him to do this for my birthday, he said he was really happy to do it, but on one condition: that Cathy Nelson (a very pretty member of the artistic-planning team) help him to dress up in his gorilla costume!"

The National Youth Orchestra of the United States of America (NYO-USA)

Modeled after his own experience as a teenage cellist in the National Youth Orchestra of Great Britain, Gillinson understood from the beginning that the NYO-USA would only be meaningful if they could attract the very best players. "The start of the first rehearsal was really scary, but after they'd played a few notes, we all knew we were going to be fine. They sounded fantastic." With an extraordinary example of using the power of the institution for the highest aims, which Gillinson considers essential to be able to change the world around them, the Carnegie Hall team brought in Valery Gergiev, Joshua Bell, worldwide concerts and television—all before the orchestra existed or a single player had been selected. Not only that, but all of the concerts sold out despite its being a difficult time of year. Gillinson playfully likened getting into the NYO-USA to making the US Olympics team, only harder, as the latter involves many more than 120 participants. "Also, in music, you always win!" Likewise, the US Ambassador in Moscow described the reality of what the NYO-USA brought to Russia: "You are extraordinary global ambassadors for the United States and achieved more in tonight's concert than I could with a dozen treaties."

Cross-Cultural Festivals and Ensemble Connect

When Gillinson started at Carnegie Hall, he had two major projects in mind that he considered would be natural developments of the Hall's great work— the creation of major cross-cultural national and international festivals, and a fellowship program for the finest post-graduate musicians in the US, to train them in a variety of skills that would enable them to lead lives not only as great performers, but also working in schools and areas of need throughout society. Gillinson and his team worked up plans for both projects.

The festivals involved talking with many of New York City's great cultural institutions. Many people initially said that this idea would not work, as New York organizations do not work together given that they are all chasing the same donors. Yet Gillinson and his team found that the people they contacted were remarkably receptive to the idea; they have since developed festivals of Berlin, the African-American cultural legacy, Leonard Bernstein, China, Japan, Latin America, Vienna and South Africa, bringing new audiences to all the partner organizations and creating win-wins for every participant.

The trigger for the creation of Ensemble Connect was a disturbing statistic that came to Gillinson's attention shortly after he arrived at Carnegie Hall; he was told that for the 15,000 music graduates from US music schools each year, there are 150 job openings in orchestras. As the standard of players in the US is so high, he thought this offered the ideal opportunity to train a generation of great players who could also spend their lives putting something back into society. The team was clear that the fellowship had to be for the very finest post-graduate players who also wanted to learn education and community-engagement skills, since the unique aspect of the project would be to have inspirational, top-quality players working with kids in the New York City public-school system and beyond. In discussing how to create a magnet for the finest talent, on which the project's success would depend, they decided that a partnership between the world's greatest music-performance venue and music-education institution would be unbeatable, so Gillinson arranged to meet with Joseph Polisi at Juilliard to see if the idea interested him.

> "Joseph and I had never met before, but we had a terrific meeting of minds and the partnership began. It's been a huge success, one of the best partnerships we've ever developed at the Hall. The two teams worked together to refine the concept and decided that 40 players in total would be ideal, with 20 appointed in the first year and a further 20 in the second. Thus, every year, fellows in their second year would be mentors to those in their first. During the recession, as part of our organisation-wide cost cutting, we reduced the number to about 20 fellows in total, at which it has stayed, and we are all clear that at least in that way the recession did us a favor, as the number is ideal. Another terrific outcome of the project has been the creation of Decoda, a self-governing group of Ensemble Connect alumni, who are now managing their lives as musicians based on the philosophy and skills they learned in the fellowship programme. We continue to do all we can to support Decoda by making connections and introductions worldwide for them that have led to numerous remarkable national and international projects. Based on their success, we have also appointed them as Carnegie Hall's first-ever Associate Ensemble. Although both Joseph and I are disappointed that no one has taken this model up elsewhere, which we had always hoped they might, we still think that it remains one of the most important projects that either institution has ever undertaken; definitely a must-exist project!"

For his part, Paul King makes clear that it is all about looking locally at what assets are available:

> "Things of great impact can happen in New York City or in a small mountain town like that in which I grew up. Every community has different resources, and while thinking about how to maximize them, it's very important to find partners who share a central vision.

Most great ideas start with two people brainstorming across a table. I often think that it's not so much about the financial abilities as the mental resources and passions that people bring to the table. They will find a way to make great ideas work within the constraints of their own budgets. One of the things that New York City has done well is that organizations and consortiums like the Arts in Education Roundtable, and those whom the Department of Cultural Affairs brings together, readily share venues for conversations, almost speed-dating for the arts, which is a great place to start."

Jonathan Vaughan recognizes that much of Gillinson's work has left permanent legacies:

"He very quickly understood in the early days of LSO Discovery—the orchestra's celebrated education and outreach program—that you couldn't just parachute in a one-day project, get children and teachers inspired, then walk away and leave them to it. He began to devise plans for teacher training which meant that the LSO could work in a particular area, help to develop and support the staff and resources on the ground, and build a capacity for them to work independently of the orchestra."

Legacy can work in manifold ways, from named buildings to lasting programs, from gala fundraisers to student outreach, from powerful leaders to grassroots volunteers. From Gillinson's perspective—born of perseverance and outreach—the must-exist does exist.

7

Evolution Not Revolution

The Hungarian composer-pianist Béla Bartók (1881–1945) was among the 20th-century's greatest composers, and he—like many others of that era—was inspired by a wide range of ethnic music including Eastern European and Middle Eastern, while at the same time developing his own musical voice. He also helped to found the field of ethnomusicology, examining the music of different—particularly non-Western—cultures and considering a host of factors including cognition and society. For music and creativity as a whole, he made it clear that "in art there are only fast or slow developments. Essentially it is a matter of evolution, not revolution."

Artists need not be derivative in learning from their forebears; it is inevitable that the past has and will continue to influence both the present and future, if only to say "Don't go there, it didn't work!" The Italian composer-pianist Ferruccio Busoni often wrote to his wife and others that we should never leave the past and must always learn from it before building and expanding on it in individual ways. And when once accused of compositional stealing, Leonard Bernstein quipped: "Every composer steals, but if you're going to steal, make sure you steal classy!"

As radically different as our modern society is from even a generation or two ago, it nonetheless stands on evolutionary feet. In addition, everything the human race builds is ultimately shaped by human nature, which essentially does not change, however much skills, knowledge and society develop. Switching gears to one of countless examples, the Apple watch may not yet, or may never have the widespread appeal of the company's other ubiquitous products, yet Apple has shown itself both patient and responsive; if the demand could be there, it will come. Their entrance into this five-century-old field represents the definition of evolution in a pervasively digital age.

Organic Roots and Growth

"All of us at Carnegie Hall stand on the shoulders of those who came before us," Gillinson reflects.

> "If we say that we must reject the past in order to create the future anew, then that's almost certainly about us rather than about the music, the art, the contribution that we can make to people's lives. The Hall's history is extraordinary, and we could not have better foundations on which to build. The central question for every succeeding generation of custodians of this legacy is: How do we use the historic strengths of this unique institution to grow organically, whilst always looking to the future? I like to think of us as revolutionary evolutionists!"

Peers and colleagues can play a key role in helping to address complex issues, if only as sounding boards for discussing challenges they may have had to deal with themselves. Glenn Lowry recalls discussing evolutionary matters with Gillinson, such as the strategy of moving staff in a new direction, how to work with complicated funding sources and when to tackle certain problems. "Sometimes the answers are self-evident but we have to wait for the opportunity to arise before being able to address a problem—larger strategic issues about how to run complicated organizations."

Gillinson treasures a quote from America's 26th president, Theodore Roosevelt—a devoted naturalist and friend of the American Museum of Natural History—that is inscribed within the museum's Roosevelt Memorial rotunda: "Be practical as well as generous in your ideals. Keep your eyes on the stars and your feet on the ground." Gillinson keeps this to the fore, being passionate about the necessity of being rooted, yet always growing future dreams out of those roots. "Evolution requires vision, creativity and discipline, and I think it is even harder than revolution; how do we remain true to our history and values while using them as the foundation stones to a transformational future?"

Louis Brandeis, the celebrated lawyer and associate justice on the US Supreme Court, expressed it timelessly: "There are no shortcuts in evolution." Quality and effectiveness are time-tested ideals, not happenstance occurrences about which to be flippant, much less ignorant.

Among the weaknesses of much contemporary art is that many artists are eager to trash all that came before. Pivotal figures like conductor and composer Boulez, when studying with Nadia Boulanger in Paris, had to learn everything about the past including Bach, music theory and history, giving him the tools with which he transformed the world of music. A real disease that developed in the '60s was the common refrain: *I don't want any training, I don't need any technique, I just want to be an artist and express myself.* Yet the reality is that this is not possible without technique or skills. Jackson Pollock—master of splatter pieces and pouring paint directly onto canvases, to take one of endless examples of artists moving naturally from the conventional to the original—first studied under the celebrated painter of the American naturalist school, Thomas Hart Benton, before moving from traditional techniques to abstract expressionism. Would he have reached that place without an awareness and study of the rigors and history of his art?

Similarly, Gillinson considers it vital that schools respect and build on the past as part of learning:

> "For artists, arts institutions and learning, the challenge is how to use their history to liberate rather than inhibit. As long as our roots remain central to the never-ending creative quest, and not a justification for resisting change, they can be our inspiration and guiding stars."

Trust as Springboard

Trust is a crucial element in being able to move any organization forward, whether healthy or troubled. Ian Martin recalls the orchestra's very real challenges and how Gillinson had to work with the organization's management team in addition to the orchestra itself:

> "He'd been there himself; he was a player and fortunately knew the orchestra's players, while they knew and accepted him. He knew how to take them with him for what he wanted to accomplish, to see the bigger picture, which was a great help to him. The other people who had previously been in that position had generally failed to take the players along in what they wanted to do; thus the players in turn didn't trust them, not convinced that the leadership had the players' best interests at heart. But they trusted Clive."

Matías Tarnopolsky—director of the century-old Cal Performances in Berkeley, California, and former vice-president of artistic planning at the New York Philharmonic—counts Gillinson as one of his key and trusted mentors.

"Clive always encouraged pursuit of the audacious idea, as well as the 'win.' He was a tireless, relentless advocate of—and fighter for—the LSO, as he is now for Carnegie Hall. This was never a win-at-all-costs mantra, but a win-at-best-quality philosophy, always with artistic excellence as the lifeblood of any idea. Our time together taught me to hold artistic values front and center of any decision, and has helped me to this day."

Revolutions frequently burn down bridges, renounce even parts of the past that worked and can take generations to rebuild. Armed with trust and vision, however, evolution can implement meaningful change without recourse to scorched earth.

Matías Tarnopolsky

This naturally applies to musical interpretation as well. History is littered with performers hell-bent on making their performances like nothing that has ever come before. Yet carrying the music itself forward, reflecting its intent by digging deeply without trying to rewrite it, maintains both integrity and ultimate impact for all concerned. Gillinson recalls one of the most memorable musical experiences of his life as an LSO cellist, Leonard Bernstein's Sibelius 5th Symphony at the Edinburgh Festival in 1975:

"As a composer himself, his insights into the music made us all feel that we were experiencing this music for the first time, yet his interpretation was based on a quest to explore ever more deeply what

Sibelius had sought. Following the concert I had to drive back to London overnight. I had an old and not very fast car, and set off on the 400-mile journey straight after the concert, driving through the night. I genuinely cannot remember a single thing about the trip except Bernstein's Sibelius 5th going round in my head, and when I arrived in London nine hours later, it felt as though no time had elapsed whatsoever."

Michael Tilson Thomas well remembers leading the LSO when Gillinson was a cellist within the ensemble:

"During one of my very first concerts with the LSO—a performance of Beethoven and Stravinsky—I was knocked out by the intensity and direct style of the orchestra and remember from the first moments specific players within the orchestra who were clearly making music with me. There was eye contact and a sense that they very much listened to what their colleagues were doing, not just buried in what the next note was but actually experiencing the music's totality and appreciating, enjoying and contributing to it: absolutely the way Clive was. Even though in the middle of the cello section, he was definitely looking up and around, clearly feeling the whole performance as would soloists. I saw the spark in Clive as someone who could lead the LSO, from his hands-on experience within the cello section and the other side of the equation with his antiques business. He was a real departure from the sort of people who were leading large artistic ensembles in Britain at that time; many were of the good-ol'-boy network from Cambridge or Oxford, who conveyed a particular kind of aristocracy in the way they spoke and presented themselves. Clive was, of course, far more direct and not beholden to that."

Jessye Norman has considered the evolution, integrity and scope of Gillinson's work:

"Clive wishes the whole world to know and experience on a very regular basis—music. He is not a proponent of a particular genre, although the great classics, older as well as the newest of the new, take special places in his spirit. He makes certain that in Andrew Carnegie's 'People's House' the sound of music is for everyone, every taste, every preference."

8

The Organization as Artist

Great arts organizations are far more than a collection of administrators, curators, marketers and fundraisers; they must be exceptionally creative environments, offering imaginative involvement to all who work there. Although such organizations can differ enormously, whether they comprise five or five hundred people and present the visual arts, literature, music or a host of other cultural touchstones, Gillinson's view is that their leadership should think and behave as if the organization itself is a creative artist. They will only achieve truly meaningful results if the staff mirrors the passion, dedication and creativity of the art and artists they serve.

Only when leaders foster curiosity and emphasize learning, embrace collaboration and truly value relationships, can organizations become beacons of stimulating work. Gillinson makes clear how vital it is to nurture a culture where everyone is encouraged to be an explorer. "Everyone throughout the organisation needs to know that their thoughts and ideas count, and our senior team is committed to nurturing this culture."

Mutual Journeys

How does Carnegie Hall gauge success? Do people genuinely want to work there? Are people excited by what they are doing, eager to back the vision? Does the Hall attract the best possible trustees? Do the finest performers want to play there? Are the reviews positive, both in terms of performance quality and programming? Do donors want to support the mission? Are ticket sales thriving? Gillinson and his staff are always assessing these factors. An ever-fascinating challenge is that, as with most arts organizations, they could easily achieve higher ticket sales and revenues if they simply presented the most popular artists and repertoire. Challenging projects naturally render selling tickets and fundraising more difficult, but they are fundamental to the Hall's artistic role. Conversely, Gillinson's view is that to present programs that no one attends, even if they elicit remarkable reviews, would also have no validity; stimulating and challenging audiences always requires an astute balancing act.

Some of the most successful as well as challenging projects that Gillinson and his LSO team undertook with Abbado, Bernstein, Rostropovich, Davis, Boulez, Tilson Thomas and others were, on the face of it, very difficult. However, by creating events and compelling journeys of discovery, they were able to generate audiences for programs that they could never have sold as single concerts. People expect Carnegie Hall to be innovative and explore unusual ideas, and the Hall has the inbuilt advantage that some people want to attend a concert at Carnegie Hall no matter what the program, because of the destination status of the venue. With so many competing orchestras, London was more conservative, so they had to push the boundaries that much more. The challenge was to conceive ideas that were interesting, unusual and important, presented in such a way as to nonetheless attract audiences.

In Gillinson's view, arts organizations have to be staffed by people who are never satisfied with the ordinary, which anyone can achieve.

"The culture has to be about seeking synergies to ensure that everything is more than the sum of its parts. Yes, people have to be intelligent, knowledgeable and skillful, but all of those attributes without creativity still make for a boring organisation. Creativity and curiosity lie behind everything we try to do, whether in programming, education, fundraising, marketing, audience development or media. I always encourage our staff to avoid routine or comfortable responses. We should also never be satisfied. Anyone can come up with standard answers; what's exciting are those that stretch us. Our philosophy is summed up for me by a quote from the mountaineer Jim Whittaker, the first American to climb Mount Everest: 'If you're not living near the edge, you're taking up too much space.'"

Teamwork and Trust

To fulfill its mission as comprehensively and compellingly as possible, every organization must work as a team—a seemingly obvious truism yet nonetheless difficult to achieve in practice. If individuals, departments or the leader want to be the star, seeking to succeed on their own, an organization will surely never maximize its potential. When he began working at Carnegie Hall, Gillinson was told that the Hall had been through some difficult times with the press in the preceding years, which had led to some reluctance to share information too openly. Based on his belief that sharing information as widely as possible yields better results and builds trust, he set out to change this culture from the start, which takes time and persistence. Some changes can be achieved structurally; for example, there was no one from the education department on the artistic-planning team when Gillinson arrived. He immediately made this change. Now all information is shared between senior staff, and by them with their teams, as company culture has to be led from the top. Gillinson always tries to use "we" in communicating with the staff, and seeks to have this approach flow throughout the organization.

> "The worst people to work with are those who want to do everything on their own; ironically some mistakenly think it's a sign of strength. However, such an approach is about themselves and not the objectives. For me it's an indication of weakness because they're wasting the team's talent pool. Fully engaging the team means that the entire organisation and its constituents will do better; in Carnegie Hall's case, we serve music and people better. It's not about one person or a small cadre succeeding; each person only succeeds if we all do."

This philosophy is hardly limited to cultural institutions seeking to make positive social change. Progressive CEOs from the corporate world have come to realize the financial, societal and moral benefits of creative employer-employee relationships that go beyond the paycheck to become genuine partnerships. Chairman and CEO of Starbucks, Howard Schultz, is among those who innately understand the value of supporting employees, manifested in concrete ways through comprehensive health benefits (even for part-timers), company stock and paying for ongoing education. The bottom line—by way of enthusiastic employees, satisfied customers and significant profits—speaks for itself. Even McDonald's—long synonymous with employee turnover—is now offering tuition assistance. Organizations working creatively on all sides of the relationship—customers, staff, partners, contractors and suppliers—are inevitably fun places from which to receive a paycheck.

Adapting to change is also part of the creative process, long the mantra of successful corporate executives and becoming ever more embraced by those within the cultural sphere. As far back as the 15th century, the Italian statesman and political philosopher Niccolò Machiavelli made clear than "there is nothing more difficult to take in hand, more perilous to conduct, or more uncertain in its success, than to take the lead in the introduction of a new order of things."

Gillinson firmly believes that we should always consider how to use today's success to do something even more remarkable tomorrow:

"I have to be very careful, as my tendency is to demand too much change, which can be unsettling; it's really important to manage the pace of change as successfully as managing change itself. I know that at times in the past I was overly ambitious in that regard. Pushing too fast can actually slow an organisation down rather than speed it up. I made mistakes when I was too excited about a particular project and wanted it to happen immediately. This is dangerous because it should never be about what 'I' want to see, but how other people are able to engage with an idea so that it becomes meaningful for them as well. It is crucial to give them time to assimilate it so that they can own it and move forward with passion and belief."

Gillinson well remembers some LSO meetings at which he would try to push things through too quickly and fail. He learned that his antennae needed to be finely attuned to the dynamic of every meeting, so that when sensing pushback, he would be able to respond by giving people more space and time. This skill typically has to be acquired through practice. Equally, it is crucial not to allow progress to be slowed down by people whose primary motivation is resistance to change. When starting LSO Live, for example, the team's overriding eagerness led them to accomplish groundbreaking work in an incredibly short time. Their pace was driven by Gillinson's wish to ensure that they enjoyed first-mover advantage; they assumed that every other orchestra would be seeking to do the same thing simultaneously. They were astonished to find that for several years they had the field almost to themselves, enabling them to establish the world's leading own-label brand among orchestras, which it remains to this day.

That excitement extends to recruitment. When the LSO was trying to bring aboard Maurice Murphy, the great trumpet player from Manchester's Halle Orchestra, he did not want to come to London. At the board meeting where they tried to resolve this, they decided that the key might be to ask Mike Davis, their concertmaster who also came from Manchester, to give him a call. Murphy's only question to Davis was, "Can I trust southerners?" Davis assured him that he could at least trust the LSO's southerners, and he joined the orchestra. Had they pushed him too hard, his answer would have been no, but they gave him the space to make his decision, also working in partnership with someone whom Murphy trusted. His first date with the LSO was to record the soundtrack for the initial *Star Wars* film with John Williams, with its incredible trumpet fanfare at the start. Williams was so thrilled with his playing that from then on he wrote his film scores with Murphy in mind.

As with any organization willing to be creative beyond normal boundaries, the LSO had its share of mishaps that are fun to look back on—with the perspective of time. Gillinson relates this experience from 1985, when the LSO made a trip to Oman as the first Western orchestra ever to visit the Gulf:

> "We went as guests of the sultan and, as there was no concert hall there at that time, we played in the large hall at the Bustan Palace Hotel. It was fascinating to negotiate the contract since in response to every standard touring condition we laid out, the man the sultan had appointed to engage us would say, 'That's completely unnecessary.' We told him what sort of flights we needed and he said, 'No problem, the sultan will send a Lockheed Tristar in which all the seats are business class.' We asked if anybody could bring their partner and he responded that anyone who wished to could do so, with no additional flight or hotel costs. We asked for air-conditioned, cloth-seated coaches. 'Completely unnecessary. There will be a fleet of black Mercedes limousines to collect you from the airport.' As he had promised, we flew over in great luxury, with many players bringing their partners, landing at Oman airport after midnight. By the time we had got through immigration (we didn't have to wait for our suitcases as they were being handled on our behalf), we walked out in great anticipation, looking for our fleet of limousines, only to discover that our luggage had already left (in the limousines), and that there were three old wooden-seated school buses with no air conditioning, originally meant for the luggage, in which we were going to be transported to the hotel. At one point we even had to get out of the buses on a steep hill so that they could get to the top, since it appeared they were only designed to carry the weight of children!"

Everyone naturally survived and could look back with both amusement and wonder. Trust and bona fide teamwork naturally extend beyond the staff of any organization to the other institutions and artists with whom they collaborate. The celebrated violinist Anne-Sophie Mutter, who oversaw one of Carnegie Hall's popular Perspectives series, is grateful that her work with Gillinson has been a true collaboration between two musicians who believe in the value of innovative programming as well as being grounded in the existing repertoire. They try to expand the understanding of what music is about, for audiences as well as musicians.

Anne-Sophie Mutter

"When I did my Perspectives series, it was such a wonderful carte blanche, with the opportunity to show the violin in its many roles in music history. Clearly one of Clive's great strengths is that deep within his heart he's still a musician with an incredible knowledge of management and how to bring music to people. He's therefore the perfect medium between an artist and audience, always encouraging artists to push the limits of what a program can be all about."

Artists do not often come across true cartes blanches, and they readily sense the openness or lack thereof in their planning partners. Mutter could suggest a piece by Wolfgang Rihm, who is quite unknown in the United States, as a coupling with the Berg Concerto, surely not an easy program to sell. Yet because of Carnegie Hall's exploratory programming over many years, its audiences are that much more receptive and adventuresome: trust continuing to play its part.

Mutter herself was fortunate to play with the greatest musicians from an early age, which opened up a world of possibilities for her.

"Einstein used to say that knowledge is not as important as fantasy, and from early on I decided that I wanted to have a foundation [scholarship students of the Anne-Sophie Mutter Foundation are supported according to their individual needs, whether for instruction, instruments, contacts, master classes or auditions] that would bring the possibilities of collaboration and exchanging musical ideas with the younger generation. We feed off each other, and the power of reinventing oneself as someone who also has to repeat certain repertoire over and over again is ever rejuvenating, as is exchanging viewpoints with those who have a different perspective."

Creativity and Exploration

While students and those on the threshold of their careers often lack experience, they typically do not lack passion and the wish to see things fresh and new, a circumstance that Mutter and other world-class soloists find inspiring. Far too often organizations try to play it safe, which stifles creativity and exploration. Two different viewpoints must be considered here: One is the artist who wants to be adventuresome, innovative and risk-taking, and the other is the possible financial outcome of such an adventure. Mutter continues:

"Sometimes I'm under the impression that the artistic side of society is muted, because, for example, there is not enough investment in the innovative and creative powers of small children. If I look at German school education, it's very much geared to subjects that will pay off in tangible ways later in life, not necessarily toward making people whole. As humans, shouldn't we be aware of dance, theater, music, sculpture and the arts in general? By lacking this, I wonder if we're not turning into less creative people. We're so focused on being efficient, which then of course mirrors our consuming process when it comes to the arts, which is why it's so important to have musicians who pedal in the other direction, to bring audiences to these foreign items and fascinate them with something otherwise totally alien."

This observation sadly applies to school systems throughout the world, despite the advocacy for more diverse educational exposure among many teachers, superintendents, school boards and parents.

"Berlin in Lights"—Carnegie Hall's first major multidisciplinary festival—became a huge success. Gillinson heard many comments that emphasized the important impact of the project, from audiences across New York City as well as from performers and partner institutions, all of whom were delighted about their participation and keen to be involved in future such endeavors. In addition, the festival achieved its central objective of tempting audiences to travel journeys of exploration across many aspects of culture and the arts. There were also two sad but fascinating insights that emerged, which identified an unexpected dimension to the festival: At one event the German ambassador made a speech in which he said that the festival meant so much to him as he so rarely heard anyone say anything nice about Germany, and at a film seminar one of the German guests talked about the fact that all of them had loved the US soldiers as they defeated their parents. Such perspectives made the coming together among so many of the city's groups especially meaningful, with every institution believing that it had benefited from participating, as well as considering that the festival had offered genuine insights for audiences.

Emanuel Ax, a passionate advocate for more widespread arts education, has always found Gillinson to be extremely open and receptive to programming and musical ideas.

"What's extraordinary is how aware and involved he is well beyond the actual concerts that take place. He and I have talked about various initiatives of the Weill Music Institute, working with the participating kids and music teachers in the New York public school system. I'd love to get more involved with that, and it's great to recognize how Clive would really like to see Carnegie Hall become an important part of everyday life for a lot of people, and not only a place where great concerts happen.

9
Management as Creative Artists

Reflecting the importance of seeking the best solutions to problems or opportunities, creative people will always strive to make things happen. The Irish playwright and writer George Bernard Shaw sharply remarked that "people are always blaming their circumstances for what they are. I don't believe in circumstances. The people who get on in this world are the people who get up and look for the circumstances they want, and, if they can't find them, make them."

Driven by this philosophy of life, Gillinson always looks to foster creativity:

"We seek to engage the whole team as thought partners, generating a cauldron of ideas. Appointing top-quality staff who ask demanding questions, creating a culture that invites everyone to be a participant, building a team passionate about the mission, building trust in assessing and taking risks, and allying all of this to disciplined thinking, enables an organisation and individuals within it to flourish well beyond what might at first appear possible. If, however, the management approach lacks discipline and structure, then the best and most creative plans—however exciting and stimulating—inevitably fail."

This excerpt from the Harvard Business Review (August 2012) makes an eloquent and compelling observation that applies to a vast swath of human endeavor, well beyond the arts:

The same attributes that distinguish great from mediocre artists distinguish exceptional leaders from their ordinary counterparts. The best leaders and artists give us perspective on our social condition (good or bad) and greater appreciation of our world, ourselves and our choices. Moreover, they challenge, excite, comfort and motivate.

They bring us closer together by providing a forum for shared experiences and by forging a sense of community. Leadership and art both animate social encounters. They can change our lives in ways that are as invigorating and real as being hit by a wave.

Whether in Fortune 500 companies, major nonprofits, charities or foundations, there are many "strong" (often meaning egotistical) leaders. This does not always stop them from being brilliant at their jobs and appointing excellent teams who also perform well. Yet this approach, by definition, minimizes the ability of each staff member to make a creative contribution; only through empowerment can the whole be more than the sum of its parts. As Gillinson has observed firsthand, there are key similarities with the role of orchestral musicians:

"Sir Colin Davis—both at the LSO and with the other orchestras he conducted—truly wanted to hear the players' opinions. He created and encouraged an environment in which the players felt they had the space to make a meaningful creative contribution. When major solo roles occurred for lead players in the orchestra, he would almost always offer them the opportunity to shape their solo part. In the old days of dictatorial conductors, players weren't expected to have opinions! There is a clear parallel here with business leaders, and I have certainly worked with the best and the worst of these in my 30-plus years in management. Not only is it hugely demotivating to work with an autocratic business leader, it also ends up being totally detrimental to the health of the company and its employees. Failing to use the skills, knowledge and creativity of those working within the organisation ultimately leads to the loss of the best talent. When I arrived in the US, someone told me that the motto for American fundraising is: 'You have two ears and one mouth; use them in that proportion!' A great lesson for all leaders."

Today the dynamic for conductors (as well as in much of management) is more democratic than it used to be, with Davis's approach far more common. Yannick Nézet-Séguin at The Philadelphia Orchestra, for one, is altogether open to and encourages the players' ideas. They in turn love him and offer consistently stunning performances. The musicians now feel genuinely engaged, which affects their attitude to their job in so many ways.

Gillinson further considers the analogies between orchestral conductors and business leaders:

"It ultimately has to be the conductor's interpretation that unifies the musicians and creates a meaningful performance, but if the conductor is open and seeks the players' creative input, it can transform the experience for the audience as well as the players. Of course, solo players do have genuine opportunities for creativity—the woodwind, brass, lead string players, even occasionally the percussion, all have solos at times. However, most other players in the orchestra have little space for individual creative engagement, so here the parallel with management ends. In management, it is possible to offer opportunities for creative engagement virtually throughout an entire organisation. However, even in the most democratic organisations there will always be times, which a leader has to be able to recognise, when he or she has to lead."

Effective managements—those not governed by fear—similarly seek the creative input of their employees, while looking to put in place a community of active contributors. Those who can combine being a strong leader with a genuinely collaborative approach are cherished. "Leonard Bernstein had the most extraordinary mind," Gillinson fondly reminisces.

"He studied, analysed and understood the context around every piece of music, both historical and cultural, and his knowledge and understanding went far beyond anyone else I have ever met. He was also incredibly articulate and very clear about what he wanted. Even though he came out of a very different conducting culture from today's conductors, which at that time was less collaborative in general, his limitless curiosity nonetheless led him to discuss the music with the players and others, since he never stopped exploring and asking questions."

Bernstein also loved to teach and convey his joy of music, very often to young people, and that visibly came through in both his conducting and how he engaged with orchestras. It is remarkable to consider how that legacy continues to this day (he died in 1990).

Straight Lines versus Creativity

Do Carnegie Hall's management and employees see themselves as artists? Gillinson is acutely aware of and has thoroughly considered this analogy himself, having switched environments from one where he understood what it was to be an artist—despite most of the time feeling like a spoke in the fabulous orchestral wheel—to one as a manager, in which the artistic and creative potential is largely an open field:

"As far as I can tell, most people don't perceive themselves as an artist in that way, yet they're aware of whether they have the space to be personally creative. A large percentage of business leaders as well as musicians are skeptical when I float this concept. However, anyone who is adding something of his or her own personal creativity to a problem, to a question, to an issue—that to me is being an artist. It not only gives them personal freedom, but is also exciting to be able to make a meaningful contribution. When I started the LSO education program, for example, the outcome that I had never anticipated was the transformation of the players themselves. A lot of them had become stale playing in the orchestra year after year. However, bit by bit our educational programs began to transform them, rather than just the kids or the prisoners or whoever the participants were. As soon as they began to engage with educational work, the players started to function as individuals, often for the first time in a long while, relating as one human being to another. It was fascinating; we found that the impact on the players was just as great as on those with whom they worked. As a consequence, the musicians started to acquire a far more positive sense of their own worth. This was also reflected in the way they played in the orchestra itself, thus raising standards."

So much education is linear and forces people to think in straight lines, which limits rather than enhances their abilities, whereas creativity is never about thinking in such terms. Gillinson makes a counterintuitive argument:

"There are times when we almost need to resist education in order to retain our creativity; after all, one hardly ever meets a child who is not creative, who doesn't ask a lot of questions. As with all things, it's infinitely harder to be a creative teacher than to teach by rote. Teachers need to have the courage to give students the space to be creative; likewise, for a creative teacher, it must be the most boring thing in the world to teach the same curriculum in the same way year in, year out. Can creativity be trained? The first thing to appreciate is that it can definitely be knocked out of you. Perhaps it is something that has to be reawakened rather than trained, because most people have it in them to begin with. The role of discipline in creativity, whether as a musician, mathematician or manager, is fundamental. Only through structured, demanding and rigorous training—acquiring the necessary skills and technique—can a person have the freedom to be creative. As with the maturation of artists, Carnegie Hall should always be growing out of its own culture and legacy, and never discard the past—to me a hallmark of creativity."

Not least among the skills needed, Gillinson relates one of his more amusing challenges regarding orchestral management, representing the people skills that he had to develop over time. This happened in his relatively early days on the LSO board, while still a cellist.

"At the time, we were undertaking a lot of work with a phenomenal conductor, a truly great artist who also happened to love his vodka. At the end of one hugely successful series of concerts we took him out for a celebratory post-concert dinner with some major donors and, after a good few drinks, he began to eat his spaghetti with his bare hands. As the room got hotter and he started to sweat, he began to run his hands through his hair, until he eventually was sitting at the table with spaghetti hanging out of his hair, not the ideal way to interact with donors! The board decided that we had to talk to him about his drinking, since this was also affecting other aspects of his work, so the chairman and I were designated to meet with him. We sat with him and his wife in their hotel room, neither of us having a clue how to open the discussion about the drinking. We had a really enjoyable conversation about everything but the drinking until it was nearly time for us to leave. Finally, we managed to blurt out our message, and his wife immediately agreed enthusiastically with us. She told him that we were absolutely right; he had to moderate his drinking. He clearly worked on this very hard and the next time he came to conduct the orchestra he was stone-cold sober throughout. However, the performance was so slow and tedious that we were instructed to meet again and ask him to start drinking, although perhaps in moderation!"

Straight lines, however, can be genuinely welcome when coordinating the myriad practical tasks involved in presenting concerts. On one occasion, in response to an unusually generous financial offer, the LSO made the mistake of undertaking a USA summer tour with a commercial promoter with no classical-music experience, instead of one of the usual promoters. The orchestra endured a number of trying sagas, yet Gillinson playfully considers that problems almost always yield far more entertaining stories than successes....

"One venue involved a huge circular stage and the rehearsal went very well. Partway through the concert there was a piece of music in which the trumpets weren't involved so they stepped off the stage, to return when required again. What none of us had been informed of was that the stage was very slowly revolving, so when the trumpet players returned they couldn't find where to get back on again. Audience and orchestra thoroughly enjoyed the sight of the trumpeters running around the stage trying to catch up with their part of the orchestra. Another venue on this tour involved a concert on a large court at a tennis club. We were given a one-hundred-percent guarantee that no one would be playing tennis on any of the other courts during the concert; however, throughout the concert, tennis balls would intermittently fly over from one of the adjacent courts and land in the middle of the orchestra. The tour's final memorable tale concerned a concert that was to take place against the wall of an old fort. We were told unequivocally that by the time the concert started the sun would be on the other side of the fort and the orchestra would be in the shade. Because of the instruments, an orchestra can never sit in direct sunshine. Come the concert, due to some strange astronomical anomaly that was never fully explained, the sun decided that day to remain overhead. Creative as always, the orchestra players went out into the audience and each selected a partner to stand beside them, so the entire orchestra was playing under individual sunshades held by audience members. The promoter never understood why we never worked with them again, despite all the entertaining stories."

Persuasive and accomplished managers are almost by definition creative artists themselves, embraced by fellow artists as vehicles for imagination and quick thinking. Improvisation, after all, more often than not takes place without the presence of musical instruments.

Balancing All Sides

"The job of executive and artistic director strikes me as the hardest in the music profession today," Emanuel Ax observes, noting the even-handedness required:

> "Somehow you have to find a way to talk with all sides: musicians, staff, board members, government officials, elected and appointed people.... You have to figure out what the public wants to listen to, and at the same time what the public maybe *should* listen to, then combine that in an attractive way. And you also have to be true to yourself. It's an incredibly many-sided profession and I don't know too many people who can fill it. I think one of the hardest things about being in an orchestra is that when you join any of the really great ones, like the London Symphony or New York Philharmonic, they're made up of exceptional musicians who studied to be individual artists; what can happen is that the musicians feel a bit frustrated because they're always responding to someone else's vision of the music, never their own. Being a manager today requires creativity to run a place with vision, but at the same time to possess an incredible grasp of detail and a great dose of realism. 'Creative artist' doesn't quite do it. Musicians love being at Carnegie Hall and Clive is a large part of the reason."

Gillinson's focus on artistic quality remains paramount, endearing him to a wide range of peers. "Clive is intelligent, funny and utterly trustworthy," relates Glenn Lowry.

> "He's changed the face of Carnegie Hall, making it more dynamic, generous and welcoming than it's ever been. His devotion to youth orchestras and to seeing the Hall as a catalyst not just for the programming that takes place onsite but for nationwide and international relationships is incredible. We've spent a lot of time together, often just turning around our own issues and problems, seeking each other's guidance. He's got a very strong moral and ethical compass."

Matías Tarnopolsky, one-time mentee and now colleague, stresses Gillinson's capacity to recognize the emotional and psychological elements embedded within most issues. "While Clive rarely expresses this dimension, his antennae of what's going on would always surprise me. It was another important lesson—acknowledging that aspect without always having to take it on."

Jessye Norman lyrically sums up Gillinson's contributions:

"Once in a great while one comes across a person associated with the arts who is in exactly the correct position to further the cause: the arts as the substance of life. To strengthen through determination and dedication an already venerable institution with new energy, new thought, new expansion of purpose and new devotion: This is what Clive brought to the London Symphony Orchestra's leadership, where we first met, and now to Carnegie Hall."

10

The Power of Innovation

PricewaterhouseCoopers—among America's largest and most successful private companies—conducted a 2009 survey of 246 CEOs from around the world, "Unleashing the Power of Innovation," which unequivocally demonstrated "the importance of putting innovation at the heart of strategic management, [with] related areas of culture such as the capacity for creativity, willingness to collaborate and readiness to challenge accepted norms also high on the list. A clear indication of innovation's move into the mainstream is that many companies now expect staff to allocate at least some of their time to developing and supporting new ideas, rather than simply relying on a few bright sparks."

These tenets apply equally to worldwide corporations and nonprofits whether large or small. Yet is innovation embraced with the kind of widespread application that its importance would suggest? Are staffs, boards and trustees generally open to the associated big learning curves and marked change, as eager as forward-thinking leaders are to embrace innovation? "Everyone loves innovation in theory, yet many are scared of it in practice," Gillinson acknowledges.

> "When I arrived at Carnegie Hall, it had been through some torrid times in the press over the previous few years, and from a few trustees the essence of the message I received was: We really want you to be innovative, but please don't change anything! Luckily this was not the philosophy of our chairman, Sandy Weill, nor most of the trustees."

Similarly, many people believe in new music in theory, but do not necessarily understand the language or even enjoy it. Gillinson believes strongly in Carnegie Hall's responsibility to the future of music, commissioning and presenting new works, which does not mean that he and every member of his artistic-planning team like or understand everything that they commission:

"The members of our team have very different musical tastes and experiences, and it is important for us to bring different and complementary perspectives to the table. I think that people's ability to engage with new music often depends on the sort of music they grew up with; we typically take for granted the sounds, harmonies and ideas that have been familiar to us for as long as we can remember, and most people find it harder to assimilate new musical languages the older they get. For this reason, appreciation can sometimes be a generational issue; many of those 20, 25 years younger than I am hear things in very different ways. At times they will embrace new music that I don't understand and get more out of it on first hearing, just as I could in relation to the generation before me. It's vital to have a team whose judgment you trust and that encompasses many varied sensibilities."

Whereas a piece like Stravinsky's *The Rite of Spring* was revolutionary when it debuted, no one thinks of it as such today, because audiences have become accustomed to its sounds and harmonic juxtapositions. It changed the world of music forever, but the context for listening to it today is altogether different from when it premiered at Paris's Théâtre des Champs-Élysées in 1913. It was then a totally alien language to the audience of the day; loud boos began almost immediately and arguments began to break out, which eventually turned physical and the police had to be called. Even then, a full-scale riot took place, which the authorities were unable to control. The world has traveled a long way since those days, demonstrated by the fact that *The Rite of Spring* is the centerpiece of Carnegie Hall's 2016 Opening Night Gala, an event showcasing the most thrilling and widely loved music of the day. As the 21st century continues to develop in endless ways, from the latest Google innovation to the most recently composed opera, such violent responses to a new piece of music are a thing of the past, although perhaps we should mourn the loss of such passionate reactions?

Resisting Change

So why is organizational resistance to innovation—despite significant pockets within our society who genuinely embrace it—so widespread? Does the fear of change come into play because people are not necessarily familiar or comfortable with it? Gillinson has considered the issue:

"By definition, it's much easier to stay with the known and tested; after all, you know it works and the familiarity is reassuring. And yet, without risk, nothing progresses, and in the end the known and tested will wither away if repeated ad infinitum. New stimuli and continued growth are as important to art forms as they are to technology or human development. Thus, to avoid the stasis of infinite repetition, you have to create an environment in which people are interested in exploring, where they also understand they may not enjoy everything, but that this does not matter. It's an important part of the role of the arts to nurture the explorer in all of us. Concert presenters such as Carnegie Hall have a built-in benefit, as we rarely present a whole programme of new music, unlike an opera house or a theater, where a new piece is likely to occupy the entire evening. Our audiences may loathe one piece on a programme, but they can still love the evening overall. In addition, Carnegie Hall's name and reputation mean that people are frequently willing to take somewhat greater risks in deciding whether to attend a particular concert or not."

Carnegie Hall's leadership actively encourages people to bring innovative ideas to the table. Gillinson has sought to create an environment in which everyone feels that if they come up with a new concept it will be meaningfully considered. Ideas are encouraged and reviewed by senior staff and constantly passed up the line. Social media is an area in which younger employees in particular are heavily involved; a range of promotional videos, the Digital Hall of Fame, an anniversary app and the *Our History: Your Stories* platform all came from members of the e-strategy team.

At the LSO, Gillinson was often confronted by significant pushback to changes that related to serving the orchestra and music rather than the short-term self-interest of the players. There was huge initial resistance to creating equal principal players for all sections of the orchestra, which Gillinson felt was vital if the orchestra was to succeed in recruiting the very finest players; they needed to play less so they could pursue solo and chamber-music careers and teach, all of which make for generally happier and more fulfilled players while helping them to maintain their playing at the highest level.

There was also substantial opposition to management's desire to raise more money so the orchestra could start turning down work and thus have more time for their personal and career development. To an outsider, such a proposal sounds like a win-win for everyone involved. However, the orchestra players' traditional and ingrained mentality was to maximize the amount of work they did, endemic for those who think of themselves as freelancers never being sure from where the next job will come. While this may not appear to be logical to an outsider, it is emotionally straightforward to the players and led to a difficult discussion when Gillinson was offered his first contract to become managing director of the LSO. Several player/board members pushed hard to have a clause in his contract linking his earnings to how busy the players were, as had been the case with a previous manager. He refused to accept this on the basis that it would incentivize him to do something that he did not believe was in the best interests of the orchestra, insisting that they should play less, not more, in order to enhance standards.

The initiatives to restructure the orchestra in the pursuit of quality meant that there were often perceived short-term implications in terms of potential loss of earnings, which frequently generated anger. Because the players in the major London orchestras do not receive a salary, but are paid for what they do, it is only too easy for people to focus on what they may lose rather than gain; the potential loss is clear, the gain often speculative. Gillinson made it clear all along that the better the quality of the playing, the more recordings, tours and films they would get, with more interesting, better quality and more diversified work ultimately yielding increased earnings. This strategy started to work and the players' overall situation became increasingly positive.

Innovative and Well Grounded

One need look no further than the gestation and subsequently universally praised success of LSO St Luke's to recognize the power of optimism and innovation. This accessible and welcoming space is now filled with activity from morning till night, replete with musical and educational activities for children through seniors, in addition to its essential rehearsal space and range of corporate and private events—all of which satisfy long-held needs within London and the surrounding areas. Innovation converted a run-down pile of bricks into a vibrant community resource.

Gillinson finds it very difficult to work with pessimists or negativity, and values the fact that the Carnegie Hall board plays exactly the role they should: first test whether they believe in the mission of a proposed project, then ask all the most demanding questions and, if convinced, back the project; if not, challenge it. They demonstrated this approach at his first board meeting:

"When I started at Carnegie Hall and proposed to the board the ongoing series of multidisciplinary festivals and the Academy fellowship program, several trustees said that although they loved the ideas, they were concerned that it would be too ambitious to implement them both at the same time. This was a wholly reasonable response, especially as I had only just started at the Hall and was as yet untested in the US environment. After I had outlined our implementation and fundraising strategy for the projects, there still remained concerns. I therefore asked if the board would agree to my visiting each of the hesitant trustees and, if I could not persuade them, we would implement one project at a time. They agreed and the first I went to see was Jerry Speyer, whose office was near Carnegie Hall. After an hour talking everything through, he said, 'Look, Clive, I'd hate for you to have traveled all this way for nothing, so I'm happy to make a donation to get you started. I love the ideas and am now convinced that you can accomplish both at the same time.' The next trustee was Mercedes Bass; after substantial testing of the concepts and implementation plans, she pledged a meaningful donation. By questioning, challenging and finally backing the projects, they not only assisted us financially, but also helped us to ensure that both projects were as good as they could be. With new ideas, momentum is everything, and with their conviction—backed by their own money—others followed. They had done everything a board member should do. However, had we not thoroughly challenged and tested ourselves first, we could not have gone to the trustees from a position of strength. It was very important that we had been as tough on ourselves as any challenger could be. Clearly, as time goes by, these issues become easier, as we have earned a level of trust from the board, which is perfectly reasonable. I feel that way about my own staff and it's reciprocal. When someone new comes in, they likewise have to earn my trust, after which I give them the space they've earned, and they do the same with their own teams."

Gillinson sees many areas in which Carnegie Hall will continue to explore new and innovative ideas:

"In programming, where the ever-evolving population of New York City will require that the Hall keeps refreshing what it presents to ensure that its programmes are speaking to and engaging with people across the City; concert formats, including further developments in the integration of media into performance content itself; education, where technology will play an ever-increasing part in Carnegie Hall's ability to disseminate and share its programs, enabling it to reach more people than ever before; media communications; expanding engagement and interaction with audiences locally, nationally and internationally; and much more."

Some people maintain innate curiosity throughout their lives, while others demonstrate the tendency to reach a certain level and then coast. Remembering how exciting it is to learn new things, together with the resulting achievements, makes creating opportunities to pursue such endeavors essential. Continuing to push forward can then transform other fields of life, as Mutter can amply attest:

"I'm 52 and still feel extremely passionate about everything that I'm doing. Even if the energy may start to drain, it's so important to remember, to visualize, the great moments in life and how difficult they've been to achieve, which then triggers the desire to repeat the feeling, to essentially overcome oneself. It's really this darkness-to-light motto from Beethoven that can give such an incredible inner peace and also self-worth. Of course, so much depends on people doing what they dearly love, what their calling is and feeling valued; it's the farthest thing from a drag to get up in the morning. This recipe only works if all of the ingredients are there, then the results are going to become really fabulous. The public acclaim and all the wonderful things that come with that are not the ultimate goal for an artist, but it's the Olympic thought that individuals *have to* and *will* do their best with what they have, to become the maximum of what their genetic makeup offers. Within that framework, I urge people to find areas in life at which they can recharge outside of their professional calling. No career can entirely give what humans really need, which is personal attention, without which we lose ourselves. I find family life—spouse, children, friendships—very important, while looking at a great painting, for example, gives me an incredible boost of energy that I bring back to my profession."

11

Serving Others as the Primary Focus

"What counts in life is not the mere fact that we have lived. It is what difference we have made to the lives of others that will determine the significance of the life we lead." Nelson Mandela's words remain timeless whether spoken to teenagers or seniors, citizens of third-world or developed countries, interns or presidents. His belief in serving others embraced how people live their lives overall, rather than the one-time donation or annual volunteer day.

The commitment to serving others has become a defining characteristic of Gillinson's management philosophy. Service—beyond the institution and always considering how best it can serve people—is liberating and removes the tension of an inward-looking focus in which personal and institutional needs take precedence.

"For me, every value system should be based on treating others as you would have them treat you," Gillinson reflects.

"This mindset evolved through my time managing the LSO. It was clear to me that our primary purpose was not to serve the LSO, the players or the staff, but for all of us—including the institution— to serve people through our music. Although this sounds obvious, it was anything but that to an orchestra created to be 'run by the players, for the players.' Perhaps not so remarkably, with the change of culture, connections began to gel between the musicians, audiences and funders, with tangible benefits not far behind, with the players, ironically, being amongst the greatest beneficiaries!"

Despite the LSO's very real and entrenched problems when Gillinson took the helm, his philosophy of service was born of personal understanding, rather than audience numbers or bank balances:

"Over my 14 years as a cellist in the LSO, I became increasingly frustrated by the attitude of the many players who were driven by what they could take out of the orchestra, rather than what they could contribute to people's lives through music. It became increasingly clear to me how counterproductive a philosophy that was, and ultimately how dissatisfying for the players themselves."

From the moment Gillinson began his management career, a key issue for him centered on changing the LSO's entire orientation as well as its culture. However, he acknowledges many initial mistakes; discerning whether prospective employees are more eager to serve themselves can be difficult when faced with words that belie an underlying focus on the paycheck and résumé enhancement:

"It takes time to learn how to ask questions that reveal who a person really is. I feel much better able to do that now, although no one can ever be 100% right. I have also learnt to listen to my own instinctive responses to people; I now understand that these are very meaningful. When I started in management, I wrongly assumed that all judgments should be purely intellectually based."

Fellowship and Fulfillment

Lennox Mackenzie recalls how vital it was that he and Gillinson work closely together and look beyond themselves:

"Clive and I sat down and worked out our individual responsibilities to ensure we did not step on each other's toes. It was important that the LSO had a managing director to whom all funders, sponsors, philanthropists, artists and conductors would relate, while more than unhelpful to have any leadership confusion as had happened in the past at the LSO. I would be in charge of internal orchestral matters whilst supporting Clive in his vision for the future and ensuring that playing board members of the orchestra were supportive. Teamwork was essential, with the orchestra's managing director and chairman backing each other; I'm proud and relieved that Clive and I never had a disagreement over the years. We worked out a system with which we were both content. This is so important in any business: It's called teamwork, I believe!"

Both Mackenzie and Gillinson openly recognized the reality that if they made decisions based solely on the benefit to the orchestra or the players themselves, everyone would lose.

By deliberately and genuinely embracing service, the musicians ended up happier and more fulfilled as people. By the time Gillinson left, a large number were doing educational work, while enjoying the more flexible working practices. Someone having a baby, for example, could opt to work 50% of the time. The goal became living more meaningful lives while simultaneously serving the music. This philosophy, however, was neither universally accepted nor loved at the start, although in the end the benefits were totally apparent to the players and ultimately valued by them. Changing a culture in which some people still wanted to work and earn as much as possible took time and steadfast determination.

What are the roots of a strong sense of responsibility to society? The answers are as varied as people themselves, yet the ends are altogether similar. Sometimes the catalyst is the death of a loved one, having career and financial success, recognizing the brevity of life.... In Gillinson's case, his core belief in the importance of serving others evolved early on, from extensive reading, getting to know—largely through biographies and autobiographies—the people he came to admire, coupled with the realization that defining and living by fundamental human values could be sustaining as well as inspiring. Two of the 20th century's greatest musicians, who spent a lot of their time and energy dedicated to giving back, Rostropovich and Bernstein, also became primary influences throughout many years of personal interaction.

The nonprofit sector is logically at the forefront of serving others with motives that do not sway with currency fluctuations and quarterly reports, yet some of today's most successful companies encourage employees to volunteer time to give back to their communities. Doing so creates tangible fellowship and fulfillment among a workforce, which not surprisingly often directly benefits the bottom line and leads to an environment in which current and prospective employees are eager to work. So why is such a workplace culture not more widely embraced? Gillinson observes that many people, including too many of those running organizations, think only about what they can gain today and tomorrow:

> "When some leaders work people flat out, they assume that they'll get the most out of them, whereas the long-term view is about developing staff and morale, nurturing individuality and creativity. If it is only about profit or success today and tomorrow, that distorts

situations and frequently leads to poor decision-making. It is vital that individuals as well as companies embrace long-term as well as shorter-term goals. A singular focus on short-term goals is not very engaging for staff on an ongoing basis."

Pushing the Boundaries

Joyce DiDonato's early experiences also contributed to her lifelong quest to give back:

"The power of music first electrified me when I began to sing in choirs as a teenager; the overwhelming impact of joining 40+ voices together, while singing on profound themes such as life and death, grabbed hold of me and has never let go. While I recognize that not every person may have exceptional musical talent, I do believe that we all have a primal sense of rhythm and a deep need to express, elements that are served so well in musical ensembles. It has always been a desire of mine to make that available to as many people as possible. As conversations with Clive took flight, our joint commitment to making music possible and accessible to people in all walks of life magnetized our passion for outreach and solidified my belief that Clive has been central to redefining an art institution's role in the 21st century. He embodies the principle of taking action and leading the way through innovation that in fact serves the underserved people of his community, whether behind bars or in a shelter. He continues to challenge all of us in the arts to push the boundaries of what standard outreach has always been and ultimately means."

DiDonato has seen firsthand how the basis of Gillinson's decisions and endeavors is an intrinsic belief that music is transformative in its own right:

"He trusts this potential, resisting the urge to dumb down or play to lowest common denominators in society. However, he takes the bold step of taking music to places it hasn't gone before, feeling that it belongs to everyone rather than the select few. For the Lullaby project, I premiered a song cycle written by four single mothers, and one of them had been let out of prison for the evening to attend her premiere at Carnegie Hall. The prison commissioner also attended and commented directly how this project was not only transforming individual women's lives, but also the prison itself. That evening, all lines of gender, race and socioeconomic standing were wiped away, as this woman became part of a very elite club of composers who have had their work premiered at Carnegie Hall."

Jonathan Vaughan recalls that the questions Gillinson would often ask during complex discussions were centered on a return to first principles:

"I guess it's the mathematician in him—that when projects become complicated with many possible opportunities, he will always go back to the questions of 'How does this serve music?' and 'How does this serve the people it's designed to benefit?' Questions like these always make the answers simpler and frequently self-evident."

Many of the world's foremost musicians ask the same questions. Anne-Sophie Mutter began her eponymous foundation to serve both young musicians and audiences of all kinds:

"With the Mutter Virtuosi and the Foundation, we have a great time both on and off the stage, which we try to look at as vehicles to give back to society. That is probably one of the high points we have in our lives as musicians when on tour, when we can give benefit concerts for those with special needs or the elderly or whomever: there are so many causes to which one can donate time and resources that give my life as a musician particularly important meaning. It's selfless and serves a higher calling that has nothing to do with perfecting my skills."

And everything to do with life itself.

12

Partnerships Based on Shared Values

"No man will make a great leader who wants to do it all himself or to get all the credit for doing it."

Industrialist and philanthropist Andrew Carnegie's words will continue to ring true in whatever century mankind finds itself, yet despite the best preparatory work and genuine desire for collaboration, failures are inevitable without shared values. Gillinson and his Carnegie Hall team once developed a major music-education project with an international partner to meet a significant educational need. The project ultimately failed because they did not share the same values. While both partners used the same words regarding values, their interpretation of those words was totally different; before long the relationship fractured and both parties agreed to end it. They had learned a tough lesson: Without genuinely shared values, no partnership will ever succeed, and what lies behind the words used to enunciate values is just as important as the words themselves. No matter how well considered any concept, purpose or plan, a shared spirit of collaboration and implementation—framed by integrity—is altogether essential. People and organizations may have worked in widely diverse environments and fields, yet their overarching values transcend such differences. Gillinson relates a key example:

> "We give away most of our music-education resources and raise the money to do so, because we believe it is important for us to serve the future of music, both directly with the programmes we deliver ourselves, and by giving them away to the field to enable others to succeed. Many organisations ask us, 'What's the point? Most of those kids or their families will never come to a Carnegie Hall concert

because they're living all around the country.' The purpose is not to bring them to the Hall, but to enable those who would not otherwise have the chance to engage with great music to do so."

Music-education programs—such as Musical Explorers, for those in kindergarten through second grade, that offers basic music skills while enabling children to learn about other cultures; Link Up, for grades three through five, in which the students learn to sing and play an instrument, and perform with a professional orchestra from their seats at a culminating concert at Carnegie Hall; and Count Me In, for middle-school students, to build audition and choral skills to open up future opportunities—stimulate enormous interest, participation and, not surprisingly, funding.

When developing music-education projects, the WMI team always seeks to ensure that it is building a comprehensive and meaningful totality across all of Carnegie Hall's educational programs, while developing those that engage and involve students as active participants, nurturing their curiosity and creativity. Wherever possible, the team seeks to develop partnerships to leverage the benefits of these programs. The resulting enthusiasm and conviction drive both staff and partners.

Inevitable Challenges

There are times when almost every organization faces having to work with people with whom it does not share values. Governments, for example, have their own agendas that very often do not align. There have been times when Carnegie Hall has not applied for government funding simply because it did not want to be driven by a different and possibly incompatible agenda. Gillinson and his team learned this from firsthand experience:

> "Well in advance of all our major festivals, we consult very widely, including with the relevant ministries of culture. On one such occasion we contacted the Ministry of Culture as usual, and they enthusiastically flew a team to the US to meet with us. From the start they assumed that they would be designing the festival's programme, which for us was not acceptable; we explained that our audiences engage with us because they believe in our programming, so we never outsource curation. We met with them several times and every conversation ended in an impasse. However much we tried to convince them that we had to curate the festival, they always

came back to what they thought was their right: to programme it themselves. We offered them the right of veto over anything we presented, to demonstrate that we were seeking to pay tribute to their country and culture, and had no interest in presenting anything that would cause them concern. They smiled with great appreciation and then went back to square one again. I also tried to point out that it would not be meaningful for them to pay tribute to themselves, again to no effect. At our final meeting we all agreed that I had no alternative other than to say: 'You're giving us the choice between zero and 100%. If you force us into that decision, the answer will have to be zero, because every festival we mount has to represent what we believe in.'"

Gillinson again stressed that Carnegie Hall's ideal situation was to work with them as partners, yet...

"They must have assumed that we needed their money and would therefore have to do what they said. Their final exasperated comment was: 'We don't understand. The [—] Arts Center did everything they were told; why doesn't Carnegie Hall?' When people want to dictate artistic policy and think that they have leverage because of money, arts organisations have to have the courage to say no. I completely understand that culture ministries care about how their country is projected, but equally, our festivals cannot become propaganda vehicles. In the end, the festival took place and was a huge success. They were very pleased and we now have an excellent relationship. It is not always possible to work with governments, and if ever we have to choose between money and control, we will always protect our artistic freedom."

This tenet holds true for individuals and foundations as well. The key question: Is a project the result of true collaboration or dictation? Gillinson is pragmatic:

"If funders seek to use their money to exert programmatic control, whether in our performance or educational work, we obviously work very hard to engage them with our vision, working to present what we do in terms of their objectives, but we never let money lead vision. It is very rare that we are forced to make such a choice, because the lasting connections we make are with people who know and believe in what we do."

Among myriad examples of needing to be clear and strong about supporting vision, so much about Ensemble Connect is about personal development, looking outward and serving others. Yet the initial interviews and selection process turned out to be less than ideal. "A few people who applied in the first year paid lip service to the education and community dimension, I guess attracted by the stipend of $25,000 a year, living in New York, getting free healthcare, and being associated with Carnegie Hall and the Juilliard School," Gillinson reflects. "It taught us that we had to be far more rigorous about how we selected the fellows." Candidates now have a very demanding selection process to go through, designed to reveal who they are as people, and their commitment to broader values including education and community engagement. As a result, those early mistakes have not been repeated.

The process for any program with wide societal aspirations must include testing its broader mission beyond the immediate benefits. Ensemble Connect is intensely attractive as a springboard for musical and perhaps even solo careers, yet the risk that the educational aspect is seen as an obligation rather than a central commitment remains, hence the need for such a careful selection process. Today's young musicians well know that the chances of making it as a soloist or securing an international-level orchestral position are small. Those who participate in a program such as this almost invariably feel fulfilled in a way they did not realize was available to them; the experience transforms their lives.

And, as Gillinson recounts, takes them to prisons:

"Of all the projects they undertake, Ensemble Connect's alumni find their work in prisons to be amongst the most inspiring, because it gives them a real sense that they are transforming lives. Most of the fellows are not interested in a job in an orchestra or any other full-time commitment, although delighted to undertake orchestral work as part of a portfolio career in music. They are committed to spending their lives making a contribution to others' lives, a far cry from the culture when I was a student at the Royal Academy of Music; at that time most students were almost wholly focused on themselves, and wanting to give back to society was a rarity. Today, incorporating a sense of social responsibility into young people's working lives is in the air, with large numbers across much of the world wanting to live by these values."

Ensemble Connect's supporters—Carnegie Hall's staff and trustees, the Juilliard School, the New York City Department of Education and many donors, sponsors and foundations—eagerly share and embrace its goals. All of them feel not only proud of the project and the achievements of its fellows and alumni, but also consider it to be one of the most important initiatives in which they are involved.

Equal Partners

Anne-Sophie Mutter makes clear how musicians thrive on partnerships. And as a violinist, given that the solo violin repertoire is fairly small, she essentially has to work with others as part of her career's fabric, only possible if everyone involved is an equal partner.

> "It's wonderful to tune into each others' vibes and learn from one another. And staying open-minded is so important, always eager to see things from a different viewpoint. We may not always agree, of course, but such differences can be so positive. And well beyond music, just as human beings. I have the rather old-fashioned theory that who we are as people reflects who we are as musicians. We naturally want to bring as much as we can to the humanity inherent in great pieces of music such as Beethoven's Violin Concerto."

Meaningful relationships remain fundamental. When Carnegie Hall presented JapanNYC, an ambitious two-part citywide festival led by Artistic Director Seiji Ozawa in 2010 and 2011, Gillinson called upon his close relationships with the Japanese business community dating back to his time with the LSO, when he worked closely with Leonard Bernstein in founding the Pacific Music Festival. This long experience led to the formation of a Japan Council at Carnegie Hall, and record fundraising from the corporate sector for JapanNYC.

Dedicated organizations thrive on collaboration. In 2013, the Hall opened up a new sponsorship category by securing support from Swiss watchmaker Breguet, which grew out of an artistic partnership between Carnegie Hall and the Segerstrom Center for the Arts in California, to expand the reach of the Hall's festivals, fostering a continued spirit of innovation.

Paris's Medici TV streams over 100 live concerts each year, reaching millions of people through working with an international roster of orchestras and concert halls. Their initial season of working together in 2015 enabled a number of Carnegie Hall concerts to be shared with people across the world, a testament to ongoing cultural innovation and shared values.

Closer to home, Carnegie Hall has become an equal partner with the New York City Department of Education, in a model of how education departments can link with local arts organizations. Paul King often considers what a positive experience he has had working with Carnegie Hall. The key for all such partnerships is to believe in the lasting value of arts education. A narrow and disproportionate focus on, for example, SAT and ACT scores and grade-point averages may well nix such collaborations. Yet those with a shared vision, with shared values, can make an indelible difference in young people's lives.

> "The Department of Education has worked with Carnegie Hall for a number of years. What's different about it now is that Clive has a really passionate interest in music education. In that context it's beyond audience development and is interesting, cutting-edge work as far as music energizing underserved communities, including those in the juvenile-justice system. And the Weill Music Institute has been very thoughtful about expanding its reach; their partnership with the New York City schools and with my office has grown and deepened. The work they're doing with at-risk kids who are in and out of our schools in a transient way, is really important in terms of engaging them. These kids are probably not going to become master musicians, but it's about keeping them engaged and in school."

Another crucial project is Arts Achieve. Carnegie Hall was one of several partners who worked with NYC's Department of Education over a five-year period to develop arts assessments for use in classrooms around the city, then helped teachers use them to better understand what students were learning. During this period, teaching artists went into schools and enabled teachers to be more thoughtful about their own work, identify instructional gaps and encourage musicianship within the classroom. King has closely considered this dynamic:

> "Teachers can be somewhat uncomfortable about having another expert come into their classroom, yet Carnegie Hall has been able to demystify that process and treat teachers as peers. It takes real humility along with expertise to make those relationships work, a truly collaborative partnership that eases the way. And the teachers really feel ownership of Carnegie Hall as an institution, so it's also a subtle kind of audience development that makes the Hall feel like it's

owned by a larger community of educators—a really smart strategy to have many such communities own what in the past has been seen as a kind of uptight institution. Together we help Carnegie Hall find other social-service work that such students need; here is another group of adults who've got their backs and can help them find other opportunities in the arts, college counseling, personal issues, so many other chances to succeed. Just to navigate New York City and put food on the table can be really tough. Those organizations eager to explore synergies and shared values help to create genuine partnerships."

Carnegie Hall also gives students the crucial sense that others care about them, since another dimension the Hall brings to this work is seeking ways to help with next steps for these kids, which the team has taken on with the same dedicated passion as bringing world-class musicians to its stages.

The power of music speaks for itself, whether on stage or in the field; Gillinson once asked Sir Colin Davis to talk to a potential donor about sponsoring music education. His response?

"He came up with a wonderful phrase: 'Even cows give more milk if they listen to Mozart.' Whilst talking about cows, I remember him saying that he preferred butter to margarine as he trusted cows far more than he trusted chemists!"

The Florida International Festival was another tangible testimony to the power of partnership, created by an extraordinary visionary, Herbert "Tippen" Davidson, Jr., whose family had long owned and run the *Daytona Beach News-Journal*. He had studied viola at the Juilliard School but took on the newspaper from his father and was immensely successful. One day he realized that what Daytona Beach needed was an international music festival, with a great world orchestra, to banish the perception of a place consisting solely of a racetrack, bikers and beaches, with no cultural life at all. Gillinson fondly shares the story:

"Tippen wrote to every orchestra in the world asking for a proposal for such a festival and got just one reply, from Ernest Fleischmann, then general manager at the LSO. Ernest sent him a compelling proposal for a one-month annual orchestral residency with concerts, teaching and masterclasses, and Tippen loved it. He called Ernest and said that he thought it was a brilliant concept, asking, 'What do I do next?' Ernest's reply? 'Raise the money!'

A month later Tippen was on the phone again. "We've raised the money. What do I do next?" The festival became legendary and fully engaged the local community, who truly fell in love with the LSO, in some cases literally! Gillinson continues:

"By the time I joined the LSO, several marriages had blossomed out of this partnership. After four hugely successful years, a new manager for the festival was appointed who decided that the it wasn't financially viable because he did not think potential box-office revenues should be counted as part of any budget forecast, and the festival folded. It is worth noting that, if assessed on this meaningless accounting approach, a large percentage of the world's arts organizations would need to close down! In the early '80s, Tippen called up the LSO to let us know that the festival had paid off its debts and raised the money to relaunch, and would we like to be the resident orchestra again. The players leapt at the offer and it became one of the great projects in all our lives, although in this iteration the festival only occurred once every two years. Sadly, it was closed down for a second time by an investor in Tippen's newspaper who did not agree with its sponsorship and, with Tippen's death, it closed for the last time."

Nonetheless, a delightful story demonstrated for Gillinson the breadth of the festival's impact on Daytona Beach:

"When the orchestra arrived for the first time after the festival's rebirth, we were very strongly advised by the locals to steer clear of the biker bars, as these had a rough reputation and were considered quite dangerous. Based on this, most of the musicians frequented these bars and struck up good relationships with many of the bikers. One night, having just left a biker bar, our principal flautist, Paul Davis, was accosted and surrounded by three huge, heavily tattooed bikers. He was terrified and offered them his watch, all his money, anything they wanted. They laughed and responded: 'All we wanted was a memory of the LSO's concerts in Daytona; would you be willing to give us your bow tie?' Tippen's dream of music changing Daytona had certainly come true in more ways than one!"

More often than not, though, such partnerships and relationships endure regardless of whether the day's business tides surge or recede. Glenn Lowry met Gillinson shortly after he came to Carnegie Hall; in addition to the half-dozen projects on which they collaborated over the years, they have also spent much time talking about a range of key issues:

> "Carnegie Hall programs big seasons, big festivals, and when they've done things in which it's clear that we have parallel interests, we've been able to produce programming, like a film festival focused on Berlin to coincide with their own festival. These kinds of cultural collaborations are relatively uncommon in New York; we're mostly private institutions that pursue our agendas separately and don't necessarily have a mechanism that would either align or compel us to work together, which is the nature of private enterprise and competition. Also, our seasons, the beat of what we do, are very different, as we all start off with our own territorial agenda of what we're interested in. In the case of Berlin, we were able to align it as we were already planning to do something about German film. Still, it is surprising how rarely New York institutions collaborate on major projects, especially given the unprecedented scope of its cultural offerings, with perhaps a handful of cities throughout the world with the same kind of opera, theater, museums and performing arts."

Unprecedented scope may be daunting, but it is also invigorating, particularly among those eager to build on shared values and combined resources. The results speak—and sing, act, dance, play and exhibit—for themselves.

13

The Benefits & Responsibilities of Access

A commitment to access is born out of a sense of responsibility to society as a whole—a belief that everyone has the right to engage with great art, be it music, visual arts, theater, dance or other cultural expressions. Those who lead and staff arts institutions and organizations, whether large or small, have a responsibility to try to serve their communities as widely as possible. This has been rendered all the more important by the fact that, well into the 21st century, the arts have slipped well down the agenda in most US schools and substantially in European ones as well. Tangible artistic expression has a direct impact on how children and young adults—and, in fact, all people—grow and develop, and can enhance the broader engagement they will have with the world around them throughout their lives. Giving children the opportunity to learn, understand and engage with music heightens their creativity, supports their overall learning and helps to nurture their natural curiosity. Gillinson makes several points about Carnegie Hall's approach:

> "We do not teach *at* children; we engage with them. They frequently compose as well as play instruments and/or sing in Weill Music Institute programmes. Our projects are highly interactive and students are participants—collaborators—in them. There are several fundamentals at work: access, engagement and the fact that kids learn through enjoyment. We also deliberately avoid labeling different sorts of music, since it's important that kids get to know and love great music; words like classical, jazz and world music can create preconceptions, some of which might set up barriers. More generally, when people who do not attend classical-music performances are asked if they like classical music, preconceptions often lead them to say that it is difficult to understand, inaccessible, that you need

to know a lot about it to enjoy it; there are many such phrases and assumptions in common circulation. In reality, many people do not realise that some of the music they love is in fact classical. Our approach with educational programmes is to develop projects so that music is music, to be enjoyed without any preconceived barriers to overcome."

As for the responsibility of parents to provide access to the arts, a wide gap continues to exist between what administrators and educators would like to see, versus what actually happens in the home.

"It is not possible to place obligations regarding the arts on parents; to pressure them in any way would almost certainly be counterproductive. If parents do not understand or embrace the arts themselves, they are much less likely to encourage—and will often seek to discourage—their children's enjoyment and pursuit of the arts. Because huge numbers of people do not grow up with the arts, such reactive outcomes become self-fulfilling and defeatist unless others—schools and/or arts institutions—take on this responsibility as part of a holistic understanding of education. Yet in educational systems throughout the world, more and more countries are obsessed by the fundamentals of math, science and language—key scholastic drivers to be sure—yet far too often they think of the arts as a luxury or optional add-on, rather than as a crucial part of education and individual growth."

Eagerness among superintendents, principals and teachers to bring the arts closer to the core curricula varies enormously. Like parents, if educators have not had the arts as part of their own lives, they are far less likely to be passionate champions. Gillinson continues:

"It is no surprise that people rarely campaign for something that they do not understand or value themselves. Institutions such as Carnegie Hall generally turn to partners—be they individuals or entire school systems—who recognize the value of learning music as part of a holistic education. It is almost impossible to work in a vacuum, so unless there is a school champion to work with—be it a principal, music teacher or influential parent—Carnegie Hall is very unlikely to make a meaningful contribution as an outside provider dropped into a school."

If, as sometimes happens, a teacher simply views the presence of a Carnegie Hall teaching artist as a good chance to have some time off, then nothing of any long-term value will be created. However, in cases where it is possible to build skills and awareness among the teachers, staff and administration, the investment can become self-perpetuating; there must be continuity about the programs and continuative people at their helm.

"Also, among the challenges of public school systems is teacher turnover. Regardless of the investment in schools, if the champion leaves, there may well not be a similarly devoted educator to sustain these initiatives, as recently happened in one Carnegie Hall partner school. A superb principal, who had championed music for many years and built a robust and exciting music program, retired and was replaced by a principal with little interest in music; within months the music teacher, totally unsupported, had left and the program was dead."

Paul King is nonetheless quite optimistic:

"I've watched the pendulum swing so many times; we have to have faith and consistently position the arts as part of a complete education, and that those who are fully and holistically educated have to have both deep learning in the arts and the transferable skills coming out of arts education that directly relate to other fields. The arts get into trouble when educators try to take one of two dangerous outlying actions: serving other content areas without recognizing that there's authentic, real learning within the arts, or becoming too elitist and thinking that the arts are only for a subset of students."

In Carnegie Hall's case, and for many other organizations of all sizes, access to schools is a straightforward process given the local Department of Education's support; they, after all, are intimately familiar with their school systems and are not only supportive, but proactive in helping to develop in-school programs. Yet this process is made considerably more difficult when superintendents consider music and the arts as a lesser or even nonexistent priority.

Gillinson makes clear that active school leadership is ultimately the key to promulgating support for the arts, regardless of individual teachers' commitment:

"The role of the arts in any school depends almost wholly on the interest or engagement of a principal or a particular teacher who carries some authority within the school. Like so many things in life, it comes down to people. Overall, the fundamental reason why there is such a variety in the level of commitment to the arts in schools is because principals and teachers are generally not assessed on this. If they were, then the picture would change dramatically. Looking to the future, there is now an irrefutable body of research worldwide demonstrating that music education has an overwhelmingly positive impact on learning overall. Maybe, just maybe, somebody at the top of government will get down to reading that research one day soon!"

The Cost of High Prices

Access to music, of course, extends beyond students, whether advocated by those working in an iconic building or an inner-city storefront. For four years Carnegie Hall was home to a festival called *Spring for Music*, based on highlighting the most creative programming being undertaken by less-well-known orchestras from across the United States, some visiting Carnegie Hall for the first time in their history. The top ticket price was only $25, with crowds not huge but definitely meaningful. Gillinson reflects on why the series ultimately ended:

"It wasn't our project, although we loved it and were as supportive of it as we could be. We worked closely with the terrific team who put it together, and they raised a lot of money to make it happen. At its inception, the festival was only meant to last a limited number of seasons. By the end of four years, and despite great critical acclaim, they decided it would not be possible to continue to raise the necessary funding on an ongoing basis and the project ended. One of the challenges in a world-city like New York is that the public has daily access to the world's best of everything, so it is very tough to sell tickets for a relatively unknown orchestra, with a conductor and soloist who are also little known. The New York market is driven at least as much by how people want to spend their time as it is by price, and even the lowest prices rarely alter the public's view of what they want to attend. One marvelous aspect of the project was the way in which it generated local pride, leading to a tremendous atmosphere at the concerts. Some of the orchestras involved managed to bring as many as a thousand people to Carnegie Hall to support their orchestra, a very moving experience. The project was a great experience for everyone involved and definitely worth the work that went into it; important initiatives do not need to last forever to have validity."

The Philadelphia Chamber Music Society is an exemplar of how accessible pricing can be successfully addressed. Upon its founding in 1986, PCMS included in its core mission the goal of enabling broad access to concerts given by world-class musicians, by sustaining a policy of affordable ticket pricing as well as educational and outreach activities. These initiatives have been a key factor in their growth from seven concerts in its founding season to about 55 performances and 50 educational programs annually today. And since the 2008 recession, despite the challenges facing arts organizations, they have increased attendance and ticket revenue each season, while presenting the same number of concerts with virtually no increases in subscription and ticket prices.

There are several factors at work here. Assuming that a potential customer wants to attend an event in the first place, an accessible ticket price like $24 is attractive. When prices are low, audience members can attend more often and are likely to encourage their family and friends to join them; word-of-mouth recommendations are the most cost-effective means of promotion. New audiences can be encouraged to return in subsequent seasons, to become core constituents and to contribute. The inclusive nature of PCMS's mission also engenders goodwill throughout the community: Private and public funders often award them larger grants, and other cultural and educational institutions are more willing to collaborate. This model is dependent on a break-even budget that does not require a full hall, and is a meaningful business model for smaller organizations with low overheads.

"Our mission allows us to depict classical music as non-elitist, an art form for everyone," observes its longtime executive director, Philip Maneval.

"Our core audience includes elderly people on fixed incomes, teachers, young adults, students, families, employees of other nonprofits and people from all walks of life. We have one ticket price and no donor lounge, and invite our whole audience to attend post-concert receptions. While we operate on a fine margin, with a small budget and modest staff salaries, it is rewarding to know that we are building audiences for an art form that we love and for such talented artists, while making great music available to so many people who might not otherwise experience it."

The Philadelphia Orchestra, which shares its main Kimmel Center home with PCMS and other organizations, has created eZseatU memberships, which offer full-time college students unlimited, free concert tickets and college-night events each season for just $25. Allison Vulgamore reflects on its legacy and future direction:

> "The Philadelphia Orchestra is moving to being as much offstage as we are onstage. Music Director Yannick Nézet-Séguin has described the orchestra as a great and beautiful tree, tall in legacy, rich in repertoire and historic programs—first on radio, first on television, first in our mobile app. We want to grow the roots of this great legacy into the community, because if you lose the top of the tree and have only the roots, it takes too long to grow that beautiful image of connectivity. Our global residency projects include China, and locally we're in hospitals and parks, giving surprise concerts, working with All City Orchestra and NYO2.... We work in wellness and medicine where trauma can be addressed by music, and within school systems, where we hope the students will grow up understanding the power of music-making to move people's lives. We're also focused on eliminating barriers and being a catalyst for communities, amateurs and young musicians, making the largest musical impact we can, both in our region and internationally."

Gillinson and his team continue to expand activities that go well beyond Carnegie Hall's own storied walls, to the point where WMI's programs now engage with 600,000 people annually, mainly students, compared with the 700,000 who annually attend concerts in the Hall. It will not be long before the Hall is reaching more people beyond its walls than within them. And while well aware that the most expensive tickets at Carnegie Hall are quite pricey, the team ensures that there are always cheaper seats and student discounts available through which ticket buyers can enjoy an undiminished experience. Donors and foundations share Carnegie Hall's commitment to ensuring that concerts and events are widely accessible. The National Youth Orchestra of the United States of America, for example, is free to every participant who joins it. Talent prevails, not a familial ability to pay. Such a philosophy is both inspirational for idealistic young musicians, fully reflective of Carnegie Hall's access mission, and meaningful for fundraising.

Countless college students, and adults young and old, have the fondest memories of buying the cheapest tickets in the most storied concert halls. Likely the most powerful example of this is the BBC Summer Proms concert series in London, where every day for the entire two-month season there are cheap, standing-room-only tickets available on the day of each concert, and lines of young people circle the hall daily in order to buy them. And in 2000, when conductor Simon Rattle led The Philadelphia Orchestra in Arnold Schoenberg's massive *Gurrelieder*—a work given its United States premiere by this celebrated orchestra under Leopold Stokowski 68 years earlier—hundreds of people lined the entire Locust Street block surrounding the ornate Academy of Music for $5 tickets—not for a Beethoven symphony but for music by Schoenberg based on poems by a Danish novelist!

Effective Stewardship

Today, artists are much more eager to engage with this kind of access than even a generation ago, by volunteering to play for fundraisers, going into schools and even establishing their own foundations. Those making their living from the arts increasingly recognize their responsibility to be effective stewards for those very arts, a progressive and positive development.

Core beliefs about their responsibilities to society at large shape the actions of most arts organizations today, encompassing the fundamental raison d'être for their actions, a significant change from previously widespread notions. Gillinson recalls only too well, during his time running the LSO, getting a call from the manager of a major European orchestra who wanted to learn more about why the LSO was so committed to its education and community programs. Gillinson talked him through the necessity of having responsibility to society as a whole, and at the end of their conversation this manager said, "We don't need to do education work because all our concerts sell out."

> "He considered that his job began and ended with bringing people into the hall and, if full, job done! It had never occurred to him that his very generous public funding was coming from the population at large and not just his concertgoers, and that maybe he had some wider responsibilities to the people without whose money his organisation would not exist. Many artists in previous days would have shared that orchestra's response, thinking that if all their concerts were

selling out, why should they do anything else? Heightened awareness of the divisions within society and the erosion of music education in schools, coupled with the general retreat of the recording industry's dominance, have made most musicians aware that they are integral players in promoting music, in promoting education, in promoting shared values."

Gillinson well remembers a one-day seminar that he and Glenn Lowry were asked to address, set up by a large group of arts organizations and foundations from a country where the new government had just cut the arts budget radically. The day progressed, with long discussions about what had happened, what they could learn from the US and the State's responsibility to support the arts, until Gillinson felt compelled to ask:

"We've had a really constructive and important discussion about many things; however, I have not heard one person ask about the responsibility of the arts to people in society as a whole. The money you had all been receiving from your government came from people across the spectrum of your society, probably a large proportion of whom never attend your venues. What responsibility do you have to them?"

The disturbing thing was that, like the orchestra manager whose concerts all sold out, they had not considered it in this way. Ironically, that orchestra was from the very same country as the group Lowry and Gillinson were addressing. Even in the US, where there is little direct government funding of the arts, there is massive indirect funding through tax deductions available to donors, thus that same responsibility to society as a whole exists, even though perhaps less transparently so.

Foundations and other funders are well aware of this societal shift. Bank of America, Carnegie Hall's lead sponsor over the last decade, sees arts organizations as a shared responsibility and central to education, healthy communities and economies. Both the bank and the Hall value their open exchange of ideas, while continually seeking to increase access both nationally and throughout the world. Far more than an excuse for some inspirational catchphrases, these programs are tangibly taking hold.

Michael Tilson Thomas finds that people are becoming closer as more and more organizations find new ways to cooperate, to break down barriers, to provide access. He relates a charming vignette indicative of this communicative mindset:

> "I could be walking on a hiking trail along Mount Tamalpais on a cool morning wearing my parka, hat and sunglasses, and it's still possible for someone to come up to me and say, 'MTT, thank you so much for that Mahler Seventh three weeks ago!' When the confluence of these things happens and you realize that there's not an inseparable gulf between the concert world and people's lives, you think, 'Yes, this is what it's supposed to be about!'"

Anne-Sophie Mutter, with her thriving foundation and outreach activities, is sanguine about the prospects for access, yet with a key caveat:

> "All that's happening should make us optimistic. The number of music students is huge, and we have incredible orchestral and chamber musicians, and soloists, coming out of conservatories, with abundant funding and advancement based on personal and private initiative. What I'm getting deeply nervous about, however, is the state of our countries that are increasingly retreating from their duty of giving our children a properly rounded education. I do wonder how long we'll be able to counterbalance this lack within our society. Of course, there are student and children's concerts and a range of other terrific activities, but very often they're brought to young people at an age when their taste for life has already stiffened in a way."

The challenge for the arts is to engage politicians and school systems in truly understanding the comprehensive value that comes with offering access to and engagement with the arts—through performances, exhibitions, educational programs and community engagement—that can transform how every human being grows and develops, and the societal role they will play throughout their lives. In the end, this challenge remains a central part of defining the world in which we want our children to grow up.

14

Mentoring as a Key Organizational Tenet

As each successive generation comes to the fore, previous norms can easily seem antiquated. Ask young people today when they think the Internet, email and smartphones came into play, much less Apple's ubiquitous iProducts, and it is not uncommon to get answers like 40 or 50 years ago. Similarly, with today's focus on educational programs, outreach, mentoring and work/life balance, let alone health awareness and modern medical advances, it can be all too easy to think that we as a society have arrived. History has other ideas, continuing to offer crucial street signs that must remain visible regardless of this or that day's traffic. Gillinson has both lived through and instigated many changes within the realm of management:

"When I started managing the LSO in 1984, many arts organisations in the UK were run in a relatively amateur way. Transitioning from cellist to acting managing director overnight—in the middle of the LSO's financial crisis that precipitated my sudden change of life— was shocking, made all the more so when I found that there were no financial reporting systems in place that would enable me to analyse the business and assess where the problems lay. The orchestra's mid-'70s manager had told me that as long as the concerts were selling well and the diary was full, we would break even. This perspective created the context for how the LSO later got into trouble. There was no real training or mentoring for management, and most people learnt on the job (many nonetheless ended up doing excellent jobs). I guess such learning at least eliminates the possibility of acquiring the formulaic answers that can come out of the least imaginative management-training courses! Over the last few decades, umbrella organisations have been created in many countries (the League of American Orchestras in the US and the Association of British Orchestras in the UK, for example), part of whose role is to develop and run these courses, and the level of accomplishment is now very high in a great many arts institutions worldwide. One of the most inspiring aspects of working in the arts almost anywhere in the world is that they attract really smart, passionate and committed people."

When Gillinson joined the LSO, some of the players used to undertake individual instrumental teaching, yet when they created LSO Discovery, their music-education programme, very few players wanted to be involved, which was understandable; none of them had received training for working in schools and, without that, managing a classroom full of kids can be scary. This sort of work was in its infancy, with no training programs yet in existence.

"In the early days of LSO Discovery, we appointed Richard McNicol to head it up. He was a successful orchestral flute player who had decided many years earlier that education and community work were how he wanted to spend his life, so he had resigned from his job to start a new life, for which he had to train himself—at that time this was not a profession. He became one of the true pioneers of this work and, along with a few other similar-minded musicians, effectively created the new profession of music animateur. This involved developing concepts for educational projects and then leading their implementation, which gave the players working with him some real direction as well as support and training. Bit by bit, more players were drawn to participate, in part by the growing inspiration their colleagues were deriving from it. The most powerful thing to come out of this experience was that it changed how almost every LSO player involved in this work thought of themselves, thanks to the opportunities it gave them to contribute, engage and succeed as individuals."

Gillinson's own mentors, particularly during his earlier years, came primarily through reading:

"It now sounds very detached to say that my mentors weren't people, but books. Yet those about whom I read were some of the most extraordinary and fascinating people in the world. It may not have done much for my social skills, but I loved learning to think based on exploring the life journeys and minds of others. For me it was hugely exciting and helped me to develop the beliefs and values that have guided my life."

Beyond his mother, Gillinson did not have the benefit of strong people on whom he could call for guidance and support.

"I read voraciously, much of it biography and autobiography, rooted in a powerful desire to understand more about the people who interested me. It was a captivating world in which I lived, offering an easy escape from my shyness. Living through the lives, values, inspiration and thought processes of extraordinary people was not only fascinating, but thrilling. Seeking to understand how their minds worked, how they thought through challenges, how they handled adversity, how they developed and lived by their values, the role in their lives of curiosity and questions, have proved invaluable."

Defined Responsibilities

Not coincidentally, Carnegie Hall's leadership team is strongly committed to mentoring interns, to ensure that they learn and gain from the experience. Most have the chance to meet and talk with every department head and Gillinson if they wish to, giving them the singular opportunity to access the breadth of skills and knowledge inherent within a top-flight management team. Where possible they are also given responsibility for specific projects, helping them to grow and develop.

Mentor/mentee relationships typically thrive around immediate interests and intentions; the resulting strengths and skills come over time. What are a young person's priorities? Is he or she willing to step outside that all-too-easy-to-embrace comfort zone and confront challenges with an open mind? Are they committed to asking questions before considering answers? However common, seeking approval and hiding weaknesses are surely not among the myriad advantages of youth. Mentors must be willing to evaluate critically, to identify and express shortcomings among those within their charge. Hard work is, of course, admirable, yet not sufficient without many skills to go along with it.

Gillinson has long considered being a mentor as a central responsibility. In addition, he genuinely loves the exploration as people develop their talents.

"As soon as I fell into the LSO managing director's chair, I decided I needed to get some advice, since I was only too aware that I had no idea what to do or where to start. Based on the high regard in the UK for American orchestral management, I decided to attend the American Symphony Orchestra League conference, and wrote to a large number of US managers asking to meet with them for advice. A few responded and met with me briefly. Just one, Ernest Fleischmann of the Los Angeles Philharmonic, invited me to lunch and gave me the time to ask every question I could possibly think of, then offered to be available to talk at any time I wanted in the future. There was clearly nothing in it for him, so his unconditional commitment in this way made a huge impression on me, and is part of the reason that I have a permanently open door to anyone who asks to talk with me about his or her career. The fact that someone so successful would do that, whilst knowing absolutely nothing about me, was a very powerful lesson."

The connections with Fleischmann were multifaceted. Here was an impresario who led the Los Angeles Philharmonic for three decades and turned it into one of the country's leading ensembles; someone with clear musical skills—Fleischmann trained to be a conductor—who became a manager; a man who became the LSO's general manager 25 years before Gillinson took its helm; and who arranged for the orchestra to give an annual series of concerts at Carnegie Hall over a three-year period. To everyone's benefit, mentoring is often a calling for such visionaries.

Gillinson sees mentoring as a fundamental part of supporting the future of music:

"What I've found—what I've loved—is to see people whom I've known and explored ideas with throughout their careers doing really great jobs, and fulfilling the talent that they showed when I met them at the start of their journeys. It's wonderful to stay friends and learn together. Two managers whom I greatly admire, and with whom I have had fascinating ongoing conversations throughout their careers in management, are Matías Tarnopolsky and Jonathan Vaughan. In the same way, I hugely enjoy ongoing relationships and conversations with many of the brilliant alumni of Ensemble Connect, whom I admire enormously. I wish I had had their extraordinary passion, skills and dedication to wider societal responsibilities when I was a young musician!"

The one thing that Gillinson is not keen on doing is giving advice. He feels that for the role of a mentor to be of value, it should consist of two things: being an active and challenging sounding board, and helping the mentee to ask questions. It is based on a mutual commitment to learning, with the primary purpose being to play a part in enabling them to find their own answers and fulfill their potential. Gillinson became very aware of how important this approach is when he had a few lessons with a famous cello teacher who thought that teaching meant getting all of his pupils to play exactly like him!

At the Royal Academy of Music, Gillinson focused almost exclusively on his cello playing: a product of the deep-rooted need to find something at which he could succeed. Many upcoming musicians today have broader aspirations, and he loves the fact that many of them are much more interested in exploring than he was at that time.

> "It's almost in their DNA. In addition to wanting to become the best players they can be, many of them want to have more varied careers and give back to other people's lives. With the kids in the National Youth Orchestra of the USA, we talk to them a lot about how to share what they've learned with others, encouraging them to see themselves as ambassadors for their art and their country. They love to have these conversations, and it's inspiring to engage with them in this way."

With the maturing of the Internet age, individuals and organizations can create widespread communities around the most important work they do, which results in genuine engagement, a true sharing of knowledge and experiences, especially since so many of those who love what they do In whatever field— music, medicine, math, research, social service, countless others— want to give back and inspire others. Unfortunately, this aspiration is not reflected broadly across society as a whole, as many people do not have the opportunity to work in jobs they love. It is much harder to be fully engaged with—and therefore optimistic and passionate about—life itself, if one has to do a largely routine job.

Across Generations

Tarnopolsky, who presents concerts, commissions new works and collaborates on a range of other major artistic endeavors at Cal Performances, became

Gillinson's mentee at age 24, when he started working at the BBC in London—a transformative influence:

> "Our very first meeting was all about artistic quality and why we do what we do, the first time I had met someone able to articulate so clearly why it's really important to fully excel and never apologize for it, to wake up every day asking, 'How can I make a contribution? How can I do better?" What we explored then is certainly alive and well in my thinking today, bringing the ideology of thought to action with concrete steps that lead to success. Clive has a great capacity to express himself in writing and to synthesize arguments. As a result, he never has to put on a game face because he only engages with things that he passionately believes in. Yet it's not about him. He always takes time to listen, getting as much energy contributing to the success of the environment in which he's working as he does learning from it."

Tarnopolsky and Gillinson would spend one Friday afternoon a month, literally talking for two to three hours. Struck by the generosity of time that he was given, Tarnopolsky would take notes and often come with case studies to discuss, learning a crucial lesson in active listening on his mentor's part.

> "It helped hone my side of the conversation. I often found Clive hard to talk with and was never fully able to relax, but was similarly never afraid to say something outlandish. He would always be very open, even to those crazy ideas, and then somehow bring things back to a more centered concept in which all the elements fit together logically. I absorbed many important details from those mentorship sessions and carry them with me—now modulated by my own experiences— to this day."

Gillinson subsequently gave Tarnopolsky an introduction that eventually turned into a defining life experience as the Chicago Symphony Orchestra's senior director of artistic planning. He offers this example as the kind of broadening in his thinking as a young arts administrator that came as a direct result of working with Gillinson:

> "As a young producer at the BBC Symphony Orchestra, I had applied for a leadership program run by the Association of British Orchestras

called Missing Rungs, part of which involved a week interning at an orchestra in the UK: an interesting possibility yet I would likely have spent a not-very-interesting week with an organization I already knew. I told Clive that I wanted to learn about how US orchestras work, as I felt that I already had a good understanding of the UK system. I suggested an orchestra that I wanted to intern with and Clive looked at me quizzically, asking why that one and responding with these words that I remember verbatim: 'If you're going to go all the way to the US, why don't you spend time with one of its best orchestras, like the Chicago Symphony Orchestra?' I said that I loved the idea but didn't know anyone there, so Clive sent a fax to its then-executive director, Henry Fogel, introducing me. Clive's suggestion became life-changing; I spent my week in Chicago, fell in love with the city and asked if I could ever get a job there. I eventually did and, while I earned it myself, it was Clive's spurring me to go beyond what I thought possible that proved pivotal."

They have had many lunches and conversations over the ensuing years, with a natural give and take centered around life and learning. Their backgrounds converged in ways that people may too quickly ascribe to coincidence, in a further testament to the universal gift of being open to new experiences and, indeed, careers.

"I had admired Clive long before I met him. Cyril Reuben, a family friend and violinist in the LSO, would invite me to the orchestra's rehearsals and concerts. It was then coming out of its dark ages and into a new era of great artistic and economic success. He introduced me—a high schooler—to Clive at a concert and we had a brief friendly exchange. I remember that he was all business, heading with great purpose backstage, angled forward as if to give him greater speed. Many years later, with two degrees in music and so excited and enthused by the amazing musical jobs I had the pleasure of doing at the BBC, I would encounter Clive on occasion at performances. Part of the Missing Rungs course involved writing a proposal for why I wanted to work with Clive and only him. I didn't want any other mentor, yet he was the most in demand. I asked for him because of having watched, firsthand and with inside knowledge from Cyril, how the LSO had truly forged under Clive's leadership a new, artistically focused direction, hand in hand with a sustainable economic framework. I was thrilled to be paired with him. The essence of our conversations centered around music: what artistic excellence means and what, as administrators, we can do to always advance this. Still in my mid-20s, I had not yet been forced to think in this way, taking for granted that great orchestras always sounded great because of their traditions, with amazing musicians pulling together or being galvanised by a great conductor. Clive forced me—and all those around him—to think about the 'why' and then the 'how'."

Tarnopolsky uses the word "forced" quite deliberately. Gillinson would always challenge him to take that one step further in his thinking, then yet another and, like many a great teacher, would ask just the right question in just the right way, one that inevitably struck the core of a given issue. Gillinson and other effective mentors have the come-what-may capacity to ask such root questions, then wait patiently—without filling any silence—for the response, not necessarily the answer. Indeed, such questions may well not have ready answers, but are a way of provoking rejoinders and further conversation, inevitably leading to an improvement in thinking, in aspiration, in ambition, in courage... and ultimately to change.

15

Money Follows Vision

When Gillinson became the LSO's acting managing director in 1984, he learned a crucial lesson from its principal conductor, the charismatic Italian Claudio Abbado, who had proposed to its board a hugely imaginative (and therefore expensive—they always seem to go hand in hand!) festival titled "Mahler, Vienna and the 20th Century" involving many of the world's greatest soloists, juxtaposed with music that traced Mahler's influence through the 20th century. Because of the orchestra's serious financial problems, Gillinson was tasked with telling Abbado that it would no longer be possible to mount the festival, and instead to persuade him to perform some of the most popular Mahler symphonies with no additional contemporary music, thus radically reducing rehearsal time (and therefore costs), and increasing potential revenues by making the programs much easier to sell. Abbado's reaction would shape Gillinson's thinking for the rest of his career: "If we don't do this, why is the LSO in music at all? It is for events such as this that our orchestra exists." They talked through the festival in great detail, and Abbado convinced Gillinson of its importance, both to the LSO and to London music. Gillinson went back to the board and persuaded them to take it on. Like Abbado, he now believed in it completely, which translated into the team's success with raising sponsorship to underpin the festival.

The festival ultimately redefined the LSO's future, and revealed for him what became one of his mantras from that time on: Money follows vision.

"It was an enormous success and became the hot ticket of the day with the public thronging to the hall," Lennox Mackenzie recalls.

> "People still reminisce about it with great affection. All of a sudden financial security and artistic integrity began to seem possible again. The LSO's reputation hit a high and audiences were becoming loyal and consistent. It was evident that Clive was now enjoying the position and feeling more relaxed."

The other early lesson in money following vision came about through Rostropovich's 60th-birthday celebration. Gillinson had heard that the world's greatest cellist was going to mark his birthday in London with a huge eight-program project: five consisting solely of cello concertos, plus three symphonic programs that Rostropovich would conduct. The plan was for him to undertake this celebration shared between two London orchestras, because neither of them felt they could afford the project on their own. This was shortly after Gillinson started managing the LSO, when he and his team were still trying to work out how to fight their way out of the orchestra's financial predicament. However, he felt that for someone whom he considered the greatest cellist in history and one of the most important performers who had ever lived, this celebration should be undertaken by one orchestra, to ensure the greatest and most focused possible tribute:

> "I asked to meet with his manager and explained to her why I felt the series should be undertaken by a single orchestra. She was very skeptical because everyone knew of the LSO's perilous financial state. Her concern was that if two orchestras without financial problems didn't think they could afford it and had therefore decided to share it, how could we take it on by ourselves? I assured her that, no matter what, we would raise the money and make this happen. She went to Rostropovich and told him about the LSO's financial situation, and that she had met with the lunatic who was the orchestra's acting manager, also a cellist, and told him what I had said. His response was, 'If he believes in me like that, then I believe in him—and anyway, if he is a cellist that settles it!' He transferred the series to the LSO. It became a major turning point in the orchestra's battle for survival; not only was it a huge artistic success, but also a positive financial one as well, since we managed to get sponsorship for the whole series, as it happens from UBS. Ironically, up until that moment UBS had only been a small-scale LSO donor, and becoming the overall sponsor of this Rostropovich series was a transformational step in their relationship with the LSO, establishing the partnership that ultimately led to their becoming the lead sponsor of LSO St. Luke's."

Gillinson relates this characteristic vignette about Rostropovich, a multifaceted man of humor and empathy:

"Apart from his extraordinary artistry, Slava was unquestionably the most brilliant performer I ever met when it came to nurturing sponsors and donors. However, at one of his concerts, which was being supported by a tobacco sponsor, he started to make a speech at the sponsor's post-concert reception, and almost immediately my heart began to sink, as it was clear that I would soon be looking for a new job. His words were as follows: 'It is a well-known fact that anybody who sells tobacco goes to hell. It is an equally well-known fact that anybody who is involved in the arts goes to heaven. However, it is a less well-known fact that anybody who is involved in selling tobacco but also supports the arts has a very good chance of going to heaven.' I breathed again as everybody, including the sponsor's team, collapsed with laughter."

Having resolved the LSO's financial problems and set it on a course that embodied its newly defined vision and values, Gillinson was clear that another vital step forward would be to build an endowment for the orchestra, which previously had no financial security. It was also important to create some space in which the orchestra could take risks. The LSO, like most UK arts organizations in those days, had no capital reserves and lived from day to day. His plan was for the endowment's annual interest to underpin the LSO's burgeoning music-education program, which was by then reaching out into local schools and communities, bringing great music to people's lives while simultaneously developing future audiences.

The LSO's appointment of the top animateur at the time, Richard McNichol, helped to establish LSO Discovery, enabling the orchestra to refine the music-education program's mission and objectives. The LSO was serving an ever-increasing number of schools as well as areas of significant social need in local communities, as more and more players became enthusiastic participants.

Even in the early days of the program's expansion, it became clear that it would be of enormous benefit to establish a home for LSO Discovery, and that this should ideally be near the orchestra's performance home, the Barbican Centre. As the orchestra's chairman for many years, Lennox Mackenzie relates:

"Again Clive's expertise was going to be tested. After much searching in the area around the Barbican, he fell in love with a wonderful but derelict church, attributed to the famous architect Nicholas Hawksmoor. The size was perfect for our purpose. There were many challenges, not the least of which would be raising the large sum of money needed to restore and transform it. Bodies in the graveyard had to be exhumed, removed and reburied. Crumbling brickwork had to be made safe and it had remained roofless for decades. It was a typically brave decision by Clive to go ahead with the project and he managed to persuade UBS to support it to the tune of £3.5 million. He also presented his plans to the National Lottery and English Heritage Funds, both of which in the end agreed to support the project with generous grants. Various foundations and patrons committed funding, and he even managed to persuade the LSO members to make contributions to close the final gap."

Although Gillinson and his team implemented many structural changes and new programs at the LSO, additional government support rarely came in advance; if it came at all, it generally followed the implementation of new programs. After St. Luke's was completed, the LSO did receive additional funding because the City government and Arts Council could see the results and benefits. Based on his earlier LSO experiences with the Abbado and Rostropovich projects, Gillinson had come to believe in the power of leading with visionary programs and seeking funding based on the energy and excitement generated.

"We almost always had to go out on a limb. Government funding bodies tend by definition to be very conservative in their decision-making; the tremendous creativity and enterprise of the arts in the UK are driven by the people running these organisations, rather than being a product of the system. The UK is blessed with many great artistic leaders and institutions, like Tate Modern, the National Gallery, the National Theatre, the LSO and many more. The artistic drive and innovation comes from those who work within these organisations and, with the best, the vision always leads the money."

Ian Martin shares his perspective on that very large and seemingly far-out limb:

"The LSO needed a music-education centre of its own, principally because trying to use the concert hall was too difficult and restrictive, and it did not contain the right sort of spaces. They found that dilapidated church—long exposed to the elements but otherwise meeting the space requirements they sought. Clive asked how he could take this project forward, with points of both skill and chance. The UK had introduced its national lottery in 1995, the funds from which were distributed to, among other organisations, the Arts Council. At the same time, the LSO had a number of key people on its Advisory Council, one of whom happened to be UBS's head of corporate communications, and we began to think about how we could raise money for it. When Clive first came in with the idea I thought it was crazy, but his enthusiasm was so strong. He had been living with this for some time and saw how it could be done, whereas I couldn't—until I became involved. We then formed a company together, of which I was chairman, to make it happen. At that time banking was becoming more and more about corporate and social responsibility, which involved encouraging our staff to become involved in local projects, including what became our landmark project: LSO St. Luke's."

In the wider context of management, Martin mentored quite a few students at the start of their careers, and related to them that if they spoke to anyone over 40 and asked if they thought when they were 25 that they'd be doing what they are now doing, the answer would almost certainly be no.

"There's always an element of chance, of being in the right place at the right time. As a manager and leader, there's much you can achieve in a structured, progressive and planned way, but also much you can act on at the moment, to take advantage of circumstances as they come along."

Today LSO St. Luke's is a vibrant place where people of all ages can be found daily, engaged in and learning about music. The BBC has a series of lunchtime concerts broadcast from there, and the LSO uses it as a rehearsal space in addition to its educational activities. It is also a state-of-the-art digital venue and the local community adores it, involving themselves in choirs and ensembles. And on one of its walls can be found a plaque appreciating Gillinson's vision and determination in establishing the venue, in which he touchingly recognizes his mother and sister who meant so much to him.

Martin reflects on the bigger picture of those with vision and great ideas who do not deliver, so that ultimately little gets done. Struggles should surely be anticipated, yet countered by optimism and persistence:

"We were always short of money, always struggling, and we always had to keep thinking of what we could do. There are fundamentally three variables involved in a given project: time, cost and quality. In our St. Luke's project, we didn't raise as much money from the lottery as we had expected, our costs went up because of unexpected problems and time got delayed. But Clive was always fantastically optimistic and carried the project through. He could see the end result, that it would indeed happen, that we'd ultimately raise the funds. I saw that and it rubbed off on me."

Jonathan Vaughan repeatedly saw Gillinson's money-follows-vision mantra in action:

"He always puts ideas first, believing that a strong, well-presented idea will find funding. So, during a project's initial development stages, his questions are not, 'How are we going to fund this?' but much more, 'How do we make this project utterly compelling and irresistible?' On several occasions when I became dispirited by the response of the LSO's board to some of our discussions, Clive would never be downhearted but would always say, 'Look, if we can't convince the LSO board of this idea then it won't succeed with anyone else.' He would rethink and rework until the ideas became completely persuasive."

Former mentee Matías Tarnopolsky finds that this mantra, another powerfully expressed idea in few words, "relies heavily on Clive's great capacity to tell a story with utter conviction. Any project or person to whom he is advocating a project receives this searing focus that, I suspect, makes his approach irresistible to donors."

Gifts to Be Shared

For any compelling idea for which a powerful vision is developed, all participants must be skillful not only about raising the necessary money, but have an authoritative plan about how to implement it and sustain the funding. In July 2014, the *From the Top* broadcast—NPR's popular classical-music radio program with host Christopher O'Riley—featured one such vision, Carnegie Hall's recently created National Youth Orchestra of the USA. This kind of national and, through the Internet, worldwide exposure made an altogether indelible impression on these top young musicians, which listeners palpably felt through the radio. Several of them spoke about their goals and dreams, about making a difference, about having varied musical careers and giving back, and about pursuing other professions. That kind of gratitude comes across perceptibly, whether in person or over the airwaves, and remains ever life-affirming.

When considering these young musicians, Gillinson and the NYO-USA team have made it one of their key objectives to ensure that the students are aware that they have been given an extraordinary gift that confers responsibilities, and that they need to pass it on to others. "The way things flow out is fantastic," he observes. "We want them to share their learning and support others. If we can play a part in developing that culture more broadly amongst musicians, society as a whole will benefit enormously from the multiplier effect."

The NYO-USA has many sponsors and donors, the largest of which are the $1 million founder-patrons, who make this commitment over a five-year period. Their names will be associated with the orchestra in perpetuity. Gillinson's long-term view is that when its alumni have established their own jobs and lives, within or outside music, a meaningful amount of support for the orchestra will come from those who directly benefited from it. He still sends money to the National Youth Orchestra of Great Britain in an ongoing recognition of its impact on his life. So many of these young musicians consider the NYO-USA to be among their greatest experiences; the Carnegie Hall team encourages them to give back and share what they have learnt with others. This represents a societal change and something that people today embrace more closely than ever before. Many now understand that giving knowledge and time are just as important as money.

Meticulous preparation for any project is essential, without which failure is likely, however extraordinary the concept or idea. The most intriguing concepts can be totally wasted without the strategy and capacity to deliver them, so having access to top-quality advice is invaluable. Gillinson considers the well-documented struggles that so many orchestras go through at various times. Does this betray a lack of vision? Could they have been better at programming or implementation? Is it just about money?

"Orchestras will have many challenges in the 21st century, one of which is that their art form covers a relatively narrow swathe of repertoire. In addition, in the theatre, new plays are part of everyday life, and can speak to many different and diverse audiences. The same is true in many other areas of the arts. Further, contemporary classical music is often a deterrent to audiences, who frequently find the language difficult to engage with or understand, and do not grasp how it is saying anything about the world in which they live. It will be one of the central challenges for new music to be as relevant to life in the 21st century as many other art forms have succeeded in being."

Flowing out of the Second Viennese School and its successors, a perception was created that the complexity and challenge of much 20th-century music made it sound as if composers were trying to impress each other rather than communicate with anyone else. Frequently, audiences were left feeling that they were listening to an incomprehensible foreign language. Toward the end of the 20th century, and now into the 21st, increasing numbers of composers are moving back to tonality, no longer appearing to think that complexity and inscrutability are proof of how good they are.

> "In general, the development of new music in the USA since the middle of the 20th century has diverged from Europe, with composers like Terry Riley, Steve Reich, John Adams, Philip Glass and their successors forging very different paths that still broadly embrace tonality. Two other challenges that orchestras will increasingly face are jointly pushing them in the same and, I think, positive direction: that their players and audiences do not reflect the diverse communities in which they live, and that through contemporary media, the very best of everything in the world is now available at the touch of a key. Orchestras are increasingly going to have to define themselves in terms of their role within their communities, as very few will have a meaningful opportunity to play a major international—and often not even a national—role. None of this spells disaster for orchestras, yet they will have to be very creative about redefining their individual roles as the 21st century progresses."

Too many organizations are driven by individual ego: "I need to find good ideas" and "They're mine" and "My paycheck depends on them." Gillinson's view is the opposite:

> "If the leader or members of a team think they need to achieve everything alone in order to prove themselves, the outcomes will rarely be as good as those achieved by involving people with different and complementary skill sets and knowledge. I will never knowingly appoint senior staff members who are not collaborative, no matter how brilliant they may be in other ways. They won't be able to motivate their staff and are bound to miss opportunities that

multitalented people will achieve by brainstorming concepts. I love the fact that all of our senior staff members are inclusive and enjoy empowering their team members."

Joel Klein makes clear that not everyone with a vision is worthy of aligning resources behind:

"The way I often put it is that we put the bet behind the man and not just the idea— someone we think has the ability on multiple levels to execute the vision, to align his team, to get the work done. But it does start with those people who have a compelling vision, which is what Clive clearly had with, for example, Ensemble Connect."

Vision by itself is like trying to buy eyeglasses with a screenshot of money, yet when framed by meticulous preparation, unwavering persistence and foresight, currency invariably follows.

16

Organic Budgeting Decisions

The National Youth Orchestra of the USA began as a concept for which the mission and objectives sounded obvious and natural. Gillinson makes clear a central criterion:

> "If any project needs a lot of explanation to communicate its purpose, you have a challenge before you've even started. There should always be a compelling, organic story to tell, so that all new programmes feel as though they have to exist. The consistent response to the creation of the NYO-USA has been: 'I cannot believe this programme never existed before in the US.' We could not have asked for a better response!"

Programs and projects at Carnegie Hall are ideas-driven, supported by strong and well-prepared plans. Their development is not governed by cost, but rather the clear sense that in order for Carnegie Hall to proceed with a project, it has to engender the feeling that "the world cannot live without it!" Budgeting comes later. Pivotal questions include all the ways of delivering a given proposal and then making it work. After the detailed concept is budgeted, the team then reviews it for the possibility of delivering it more efficiently and cost-effectively. Gillinson describes the gestation of Ensemble Connect:

> "Our original concept was for a far bigger project, up to 90 fellows so that they could also function as an orchestra. However, after our initial analysis we decided that this would be far too expensive, so we reconceived the project and brought the number down to 40 fellows, launching the programme in January of 2007. When the recession hit in 2008, we had to look for ways to make major cuts across our entire organisation. This included significant reductions to some programmes and cutting others altogether. We were clear that

we had to keep Ensemble Connect, so we examined every possible adjustment and decided to bring it down from 40 to 20 fellows. This meant eliminating the yearly staggering on which the original concept was based, whereby 20 new fellows joined each year, with the 20 second-year fellows mentoring them. Our review convinced us that we could still deliver the whole mission, and we are delighted that the redesign is now even better than the original, with a much more meaningful community created, who spend the entire two years together. The review also highlighted the fact that we would have an ever-increasing number of alumni going out into the world living their lives based on the Ensemble's performance, education and community-engagement mission, so a larger programme would become less important as time went by."

Adaptation is key. The team managed through the recession to make the program better, more refined, tighter in every way and more successful. Financial pressures can place decidedly good demands on both teams and plans, which is a matter of organizational culture. During the 2008 global financial crisis and subsequent recession, Gillinson and his team took what could have been a period of utter panic and applied the creative skills gleaned from the near-constant struggles in his early days at the LSO:

"We could have chopped everything by 20%, yet that would have been ridiculous as well as destructive. We would have damaged many projects of real value, and perhaps kept things that needed to change or even be dropped. Instead, we all worked very closely to find ways to transform everything we did. The criteria I set were that we should reduce our budget overall by about 20%, yet do it in such a way as to be invisible to anyone but ourselves, whilst doing everything in our power not to lose any staff. Thanks to the team, we achieved these objectives and, through this, built a far better business model for the Hall's future. We have a great team and I knew that by working together we would not only survive, but also create an even more extraordinary future. The defining moment for all of us was at the annual press conference to launch our 2009-2010 season, which took place at the end of January 2009; this would test whether we had succeeded in making all of our changes invisible. In my speech I noted that we had cut our operating budget from $84 million to $70 million in response to the financial crisis, and one of the most widely read music journalists asked: 'Please could you tell us where the cuts are? I cannot tell the difference from last year.' We never even had to pay him to ask this!"

The staff's objectives—to make the cuts invisible and not lose any employees—were extremely motivating. Gillinson adds a central caveat:

"It is important to be aware that one cannot do that same exercise twice. If we had to make another such major budget cut, we would not be able to do it invisibly again, because once you've trimmed everything to the best of your ability, the same opportunities no longer exist. The recession made it clear that even the best-run organisations, over time, get comfortable. One of the most important lessons we learnt was not just in the immediate response to it, but also in trying to ensure that the rigor we used in making the cuts continues to inform the way we run the business going forward."

Unpredictability

When something like a recession hits, do even experienced, perceptive leaders and teams really know the answers? Gillinson is frank.

"When a crisis strikes, the chances are that you initially have no idea what to do. Organisations can either respond mechanistically or work collaboratively to find creative solutions. It is not a failing not to know the answers immediately; what matters is the process for addressing the challenges. In addition, trying to eliminate risk will almost certainly lead to conservative answers that will diminish the purpose of the institution and to a reduction in its appeal to donors, audiences and the media. This speaks to my view that the greatest risk of all is trying to avoid risk! This can be a difficult balance to achieve and must be addressed by answering crucial questions: What are the objectives of every single program? How do we stay true to everything we believe in? How do we restructure plans or rethink them while still maintaining our mission, values and objectives? However onerous, such questions must be answered as directly and openly as possible. Across-the-board cuts can be both devastating and shortsighted, and can cause irreversible damage. Yet approached programme by programme and aspect by aspect, improvements can be made concurrently with reductions, and a large number of incremental improvements can achieve as much as major cuts. Those afraid to go through these pains may well cause an organisation to break down, close or merge."

Whether at a major institution such as Carnegie Hall or the two-person nonprofit occupying a small office, funding sources are rarely if ever predictable. Managers know how much they have taken in over previous years, but organizations have to win renewed support every year. And, of course, they have to garner it based on the programs themselves: Less excitement inevitably leads to less incoming money.

The money, employment and economic impact, however, are clearly there. Americans for the Arts, through its *Creative Industries: Business & Employment in the Arts* reports, shares telling statistics (as of January 2015):

"Nationally, 702,771 businesses are involved in the creation or distribution of the arts, and they employ 2.9 million people. This represents 3.9 percent of all U.S. businesses and 1.9 percent of all U.S. employees—demonstrating statistically that the arts are a formidable business presence and broadly distributed across our communities. Arts businesses and the creative people they employ stimulate innovation, strengthen America's competitiveness in the global marketplace, and play an important role in building and sustaining economic vibrancy."

Trust

This is a budget element every bit as tangible and necessary as the bank balance to cover the week's payroll. If audiences, donors and boards see management and staff delivering the mission on budget, year after year, they are much more inclined to support new initiatives. And when the inevitable difficulties arise, how an organization responds reveals a great deal about its culture. Gillinson has carefully considered the central nature of trust over the years, often brought to the fore by good or bad financial decisions, yet as broadly applicable as anything in life.

"I have to earn the trust of the people I ultimately report to: the board. My senior staff has to earn my trust, and their staff has to earn their trust. This should be a basic part of any company culture. I am extremely lucky to have a great senior team and they have totally earned my trust, so I am able to give them all a lot of space. Trust is not just about doing a great job, but the knowledge that people will come and talk about a problem as soon as it arises. Trust also means that if staff members come to you with a problem, you won't bite their head off or fire them. With a positive company culture, the staff knows that it's safe to raise problems straightaway and talk about rather than hide them. The most important thing about mistakes, alongside acknowledging and dealing with them as quickly as possible, is to make sure we don't make the same mistake twice!"

Trust naturally extends to whether a person's focus is consistently directed inward for self-gain, or outward on behalf of those he or she serves. Ian Martin, whose career has put him in contact with many corporate leaders, reflects:

"When I was involved with the bank, we interacted with many organisations, including the LSO, and we were always impressed by the ability of Clive and other managers to be able to succeed, often against the odds. Their focus was always on trying to make decisions work for the larger community, whereas people in big corporations— focused on 'doing it for me'—managed to fail even though they had everything."

Jonathan Vaughan shares a perspective that highlights the perpetual advantages of listening and perseverance, both in securing funding as well as in making core budget decisions:

"When Clive is looking to secure funding for a project, he will spend a great deal of time talking to potential supporters about their interests before presenting his own ideas. On a number of occasions, in long meetings apparently heading nowhere, I've seen him suddenly turn things around by picking up on a chance remark by a funder in the last five minutes of the meeting, and having the flexibility and quick thinking to figure out how the funder's interests can be met without compromising his own position. You can, of course, only do this if you fully understand the strengths and weaknesses of your own organisation, whilst knowing how to adapt your resources."

Sound budget decisions that closely fit together, each seen as necessary components of the whole, go a long way in creating harmony for all concerned.

17

Managing & Encouraging Well-Considered Risk

The word "risk" conjures up all manner of reckless behavior; responsible people, after all, generally try to avoid risky activities, as these are often associated with pain, financial loss, unemployment, eviction or a host of other pitfalls. Yet where would we be as a society, as a culture, as people, without *well-considered* risk?

Steven Kotler, in a 2012 *Forbes* magazine article, "Einstein at the Beach: The Hidden Relationship Between Risk and Creativity," makes fundamental observations about their interconnectedness:

> "From a neurological perspective, creativity is the product of the brain making long-distance connections. Most of the time, when we think about a problem, the database the brain searches for a solution is narrow. This helps us from getting swamped by data. If you're trying to solve a marketing problem, remembering what Aunt Helga said on your third birthday isn't much help. But when creatives problem-solve, they don't just search the familiar databases, they stretch their brains hunting for dimmer connections, subtler relationships, novel linkages. When we're creative, Aunt Helga might actually be of some assistance. When the brain encounters unfamiliar stimuli under uncertain conditions—especially when those are dangerous—baser instincts take over. As a result, the brain's rational extrinsic system is shunted aside in favor of the intuitive creative system. Risk, therefore, causes the mind to stretch its muscles. It creates mandatory conditions for innovation. It trains the brain to think in unusual ways [...] and be more creative."

Most arts organizations have people with the ability and imagination to develop bold new ideas. However, Gillinson finds that fear of failure often inhibits their actions, leading to 'safety first' decisions, when only by engaging with innovative ideas will they inspire those around them.

"Trying to avoid risk inevitably leads organisations to seek safe, comfortable decisions, instead of developing exciting and challenging ideas, without which it is almost impossible to generate the inspiration that audiences, donors, trustees and staff seek and respond to. Whether as individual human beings or as institutions, we have to take risks if we are going to keep developing. If not, we stagnate. The issue for arts institutions (and people!) is not whether to take risks or not, but how best to evaluate and manage them."

Gillinson learned to listen to his instincts early on in his life as a manager:

"In my very early days as managing director of the LSO, a distinguished and experienced manager proposed a major artistic concept to me. He was convinced that it would be a huge success, and even though the concept did not excite me, I assumed that, as he knew so much and I knew so little, he must be right, so I agreed to take it on. It was not a success, which may or may not have been our fault, but the fundamental lesson I learned is that it's impossible to engage other people with an idea if you don't believe in it yourself. That has been an absolute rule for me from that day onward."

Gillinson has always shared his instincts within the context of encouraging his teams to be free and unafraid to put their own ideas forward, while well aware that leading by example is also essential. In the few years prior to his arrival at Carnegie Hall, it had been through some major challenges, which among other things had led to substantial staff turnover. The Hall had also found itself regularly in the press beyond the concerts and programs themselves, which led to a more defensive, inward-looking culture. Part of Gillinson's challenge was to once again engage the team with innovation and openness. In 2003, the reported merger with the New York Philharmonic was seen as something of a savior, a source of stability as reported by *The New York Times*:

"In a surprising cultural merger, the New York Philharmonic has agreed to move to Carnegie Hall, leaving Lincoln Center.... The move back to Carnegie Hall, where the orchestra had historically resided on West 57th Street, could come as soon as 2006, more than 40 years after it left and became an anchor of Lincoln Center."

In the end, the merger was abandoned and by the time they brought Gillinson aboard in 2005, Carnegie Hall's staff and board were not only ready but hungry to be open and creative, to move on from their recent problems and seek new horizons.

Gillinson remains frank about his own motivations:

"I cannot live without new challenges, new ideas, change. If my job ever starts to get comfortable, I get bored and can almost feel my energy seeping away. To remain energised and excited we have to be constantly testing ourselves and exploring new ideas, so that every hour of every day we know that anything less than creative solutions is not good enough. After a particularly routine concert at the LSO many years ago, the concertmaster crushingly described the performance as 'one for the mortgage.' Reverting to automatic pilot is the beginning of the end in the arts. Of course, we are extremely lucky to be working in an area of life where the outcomes of what we do, as well as the cultures in which we work, are totally conducive to becoming lifelong learners, so the avoidance of routine in any performance is vital: better to do one less performance than a dull one. For all great artists, the performance they are doing is the most important of their lives or they should not be doing it."

Ideas-Driven Approach

Well-considered risk by definition minimizes risk without eliminating it. As Gillinson outlines:

"Everything we do is driven by ideas that we love. A good idea is never good enough; unless we are truly excited, how will we ever excite anyone else about it? Assessing and then managing the risks is a vital part of the process of developing any new project, but it never comes first. A primary lens through which we judge every new project is, 'Can the world live without it'? The NYO-USA is a perfect example. When we launched it, the almost universal response was that people could not believe it did not already exist; they thought it so important that it must have been around forever."

The desire to work collaboratively and a willingness to invest in the future—balancing people and finances—have repeatedly been shown throughout history to be key links, not only in overcoming very real problems and abounding risk, but continuing to move ahead. In 1929, on the cusp of the Great Depression, Marjorie Post's Postum Company made a large acquisition, paying $22 million for the majority of Clarence Birdseye's General Foods Company. The following few years were spent on stabilizing its business but then it quickly expanded, buying the rest of General Foods then Sanka Coffee and others, all while its competitors generally retrenched. Four generations later, most people who invested anywhere near the height, depth or width of the 2008 Great Recession made spectacular returns in a remarkably short time. Yet whether confronted by internal or external problems, managements more often than not think that the most important thing is to try to avoid risk. Gillinson's view is that risk is fundamental to every business and, in fact, to every aspect of life.

History is a great teacher and often a powerful motivator, yet because something did not work 10 years ago does not mean that it will not work today. When Gillinson first suggested the idea of multidisciplinary festivals at Carnegie Hall, which would involve engaging with other leading cultural institutions throughout New York City, the general response was that its cultural organizations do not work together as they are all chasing the same donors, so there was little chance that this idea would fly. Gillinson nonetheless went and spoke to a few leaders, who loved the idea and agreed to participate.

> "These partnerships have been a huge success because by working together we have created projects that amount to more than the sum of the individual parts, and every participating organisation benefits. Received wisdom is always worth testing and is not necessarily wisdom! The key is to be guided by the conviction that an unmissable idea has to happen, followed by rigorously working out how to implement it. Risk assessment should only come once the idea and its implementation strategy have been clearly formulated."

Is it a coincidence that so many of the projects that Gillinson and his collaborators have taken on became home runs? LSO St. Luke's, LSO Live, LSO Discovery, national and international festivals, Ensemble Connect, NYO-USA, NYO2, Carnegie Hall's Resnick Education Wing… The list continues to grow and Gillinson has carefully considered the issue.

"Each of these projects was high risk when we embarked on it. On top of developing 'irresistible ideas', it is vital to have a team with the confidence and rigor to think through effective and efficient implementation, as well as how to assess and minimise risk. Nonetheless, at some point you still have to jump. With the NYO-USA, for example, we decided that the best way to test potential support for the project and simultaneously create a launch pad for it would be to create a group of founder-patrons. We relatively quickly recruited several, giving us a substantial five-year underpinning, although not fully covering the annual costs of about $2.5 million. However, it was a great indicator of donors' response to the concept, and sufficient to give us the confidence to launch. Whilst it is theoretically possible to try and raise in advance all the money needed to sustain a new project, it may well take years to get there, with a strong chance that the enthusiasm will have dissipated before you get there. It is also far easier to raise support for a project that is flying than to do so for an as-yet-untried concept. For example, one NYO-USA donor thought it was a bad idea when first we raised the concept with the board and only came in afterwards, once he had seen the orchestra in action and registered the extraordinary public and media acclaim it received. He now thinks it is one of the best things we've ever done."

In large pockets of society, however, there remains a palpable aversion to even well-considered risk that can become stultifying. For instance, public servants are far too often judged on their failures rather than on their ability to make important decisions that move society forward, which by definition involve taking risks. By simply maintaining the status quo and avoiding media headlines, they can be perceived to be doing a good job, even if in reality they have achieved little. People with responsibility for spending public money tend to be scared of making even the hint of a wrong choice, hence gravitating toward safe options; government employees rarely lose their jobs for playing it safe. The extreme is in totalitarian societies, where those who take a risk and fail can face debilitating consequences. To be sure, those entrusted with public money must be careful; finding that balance is never easy. Taking a risk and failing can be painfully hard to swallow for those without the courage to live with the occasional failure, or those whose bosses will not accept mistakes.

Beyond the Status Quo

Joel Klein considers any vision without an element of risk is often not worth pursuing: It may have been done before and is perhaps boring or lacking excitement. "And although one doesn't want to include high-wire acts, balancing well-informed projects with their risks is something that Clive is clearly able to do, while at the same time not pursuing those that are impulsive or unfounded." Conversely, Gillinson often found it immensely frustrating dealing with the Arts Council in the UK, as they used the rhetoric of backing excellence, but usually ended up making formulaic decisions out of fear of criticism.

Paul King relates that—whatever the project—they always like to hold it up to the light and examine it from different perspectives, while engaging a larger community in that conversation. Although a given project may still fail, doing that kind of due diligence is essential:

> "What I find engaging in our schools and teachers, and among my own staff, is that projects not so tightly constrained or just a replication of something that's previously happened, can produce great excitement and are worth capturing, despite the risks that may be involved. It's challenging within larger bureaucracies, as by their very nature they're not so willing to take risks."

These kinds of initiatives continue to grow, yet how can society as a whole effectively deal with not meeting hopefully high expectations when it comes to the wide-ranging benefits of arts education? Anne-Sophie Mutter well understands the risk of its avoidance:

> "My own view about such risk, and of course we're not talking about neurosurgery or heart surgery here, is that it may alter the ego. Herbert von Karajan used to say that if you've reached all your goals, you've probably chosen them on too low a level. Risk-taking is absolutely essential. If I look at Roger Federer, with his one-handed backhand, it's clearly a dying-out way of playing tennis because it's the more risk-taking, the more elegant, the more difficult to control, *but...* it's so incredible when it works, seemingly effortless and so effective. It would give any of us pleasure to reach that. The question in life, when you take risk, is to find the balance. That's why I'm so passionate about contemporary music, because I always feel the risk of failure, of not being able to pull it off. That somehow triggers in

me a great appetite to prove to myself that my boundaries can be expanded. I do feel that we should always leave our comfort zone behind, but it's not within everyone's makeup to leave that space."

Glenn Lowry considers how Carnegie Hall has been a beacon for 125 years and that we as a society expect our cultural centers to be here for the long-term. The key is to balance the risks against the responsibility to a larger set of goals.

"That's the fine line between how much risk you can take on while at the same time ensuring the long-term stability of your institution. To look at the original list of Fortune 500 companies, for example, against those which remain today, is shocking. Yet looking at the cultural institutions that were in New York before 1900, it's equally astounding because most of them are still here!"

There are firm reasons why Carnegie Hall will be celebrating its 200th anniversary on May 5, 2091. Avoiding risk, particularly that which is well-considered and supported by a strongly creative and cohesive team, more often than not represents the real reckless behavior.

18
The Role of Media

Long a media visionary, Michael Tilson Thomas has carefully considered its ongoing role within the spheres of music, culture and society:

"We still have a long way to go. What I don't know is how much of a public there is for some of the things we make, such as the filming of concerts. One of the things I'm trying to do with the New World Symphony is to invent a new kind of genre, more along the lines of an art installation, an environment in which music plays a part and is therefore consumed in a different way than currently typical—to encourage and challenge young musicians to imagine concert experiences in which they can effectively communicate with audiences... to think about those things and actually make them come about. There are always reasons not to do something: too expensive, too complicated, too time-consuming, so it's really necessary to come up with ideas that aren't necessarily coming from management but rather emerging from the ensemble itself, which creates a sense of involvement from all concerned. In my own case, it sometimes took decades for technology to catch up with the dreams I had for music, while young people today have no idea of a world without this cutting-edge technology. I have great faith in them to move music forward, which is also something that Clive is looking to do with the young groups and ensembles that he works with, to get them to be more imaginative about what they're doing, where they do it and with whom they collaborate—so important for the future."

The adept use of media in all of its forms and functions, by organizations of every size and influence, has remained crucial for eons. Whether from 18th-century newspapers, the earliest advertising agencies in the 19th, mass-marketing national chain stores in the 20th or social media today, how to capture the imagination has been the age-old question.

Gillinson comments on the continuing quest for meaningful contemporary answers:

"An important part of the picture is access and seeking to ensure that people who cannot attend our concerts in person can nonetheless experience them in as meaningful a way as possible. At the LSO we negotiated an unprecedented deal with the BBC to broadcast a large number of our Barbican concerts on the radio each year, as well as seeking other means of disseminating our presentations. This included the creation of our own recording label, LSO Live, for which a primary driver was to share our core musical offerings as widely as possible, at a price that was low enough to enable them to be a whim rather than a considered purchase. We wanted the decision to be as easy as buying a pint of beer. We created and launched the label despite having no one on staff with an in-depth knowledge of the recording business. I appointed a young member of the marketing department, Chaz Jenkins, to run it; he was fascinated by the recording business and thrilled about the opportunity to develop our own label. Whilst we could theoretically have recruited someone from a recording company, I deliberately avoided that route as I felt that the recording companies were themselves struggling to address the challenges of a rapidly changing marketplace. I wanted someone who could approach this initiative with fresh eyes and ears. Chaz did a brilliant job and from early on LSO Live became the leading orchestra-owned label, and remains so to this day. At Carnegie Hall, we combine a significant radio broadcasting partnership with WQXR with a complementary webcasting partnership with Medici. tv, thus sharing many performances with substantial audiences worldwide. In the coming years we will continue to expand our dissemination of performances and education content using multiple digital platforms. This will include sharing skills, knowledge and programmes from which people can learn and grow. In addition, interaction and engagement with audiences is in its relatively early days, and will be an ever-growing part of our e-strategy."

Social media, of course, continues its lightning rise, with implications as far-reaching as they are wide-ranging, and Carnegie Hall actively engages with all of the leading social-media platforms. Gillinson recognizes that this is an area largely understood and inhabited by the younger staff, who engage with it on an ongoing basis. As a result, Carnegie Hall offers them significant freedom, understanding that trying to control everything within the social-media space would be antithetical to how that space works. It requires fluidity, creativity and spontaneity, together with the ability to take its daily pulse. Gillinson actively embraces new technologies, but only on the understanding that they have to serve the music and not the other way around; he tries to ensure that each project in every area of Carnegie Hall's work is mission driven. He is also clear that media developments, although seen by many as a threat, will offer unprecedented opportunities to the arts, increasingly giving people across the globe access to, and possibilities for, engagement with great art of every kind: an ever more powerful democratizing force.

Among the challenges is dealing with less newspaper space for arts and culture because newspapers are struggling with an increasingly uncertain business model. Another is that a concert happens only once; its review is by definition retrospective, unless a given performance is part of a series. Media standards are another issue. Longtime concertgoers have empyrean benchmarks by which they judge all concerts, yet reviewers can all too easily fall back to earth. Gillinson considers the difficulties:

> "*The New York Times* still has a strong team of music writers on staff, yet worldwide there are diminishing numbers of journalists covering events for the established media, leading to a continuing erosion of arts coverage, substantially due to budgetary constraints. In addition, the mainstream media, in order to control staff costs, are increasingly using freelance writers. Alongside this falloff in coverage by the more established media, there are ever-increasing numbers of independent bloggers writing about music and the arts, but the challenge for the public is that they don't have benchmarks to determine who is worth reading in this largely unregulated space."

There are two central issues that engage Gillinson: how to drive revenues out of media where this is meaningful and relevant, and trying to understand all the implications of the current environment, in which the availability of infinite amounts of content and information online (largely free) creates a huge challenge for the public. How does one select or even find what is good and what is not? How to separate the wheat from the chaff? How to avoid the boredom of sifting through mountains of information and content, much of it mediocre at best?

After all, infinite choice has now become almost as big a challenge as lack of choice. The free market has begun to answer some of these questions with likes, dislikes, stars and other representations, and organizations have the opportunity to build up what is successful with a passionate following. Gillinson sees major opportunities for Carnegie Hall as a curator in the new-media spaces as it is in the concert hall: capitalizing on the fact that online there are none of the limitations of having a defined concert venue in a fixed physical location at a particular time in history.

Journalists focused on a particular story, and spending time with cultural organizations at home or on tour, will often write informative articles based on direct, extended observation—a far cry from today's increasingly automated fast-food culture. In his days at the LSO, Gillinson grew to enjoy working with the media, and the LSO players were excellent at engaging with them, always briefed to communicate the orchestra's mission and plans.

Dvora Lewis, known as the UK's Queen of Music PR, for nearly four decades counted the LSO among her primary clients and worked side by side with Gillinson through the orchestra's trials, crises and successes, as well as with its celebrated conductors including Bernstein, Davis, Previn, Tilson Thomas and Rostropovich.

Dvora Lewis

"Communicating with everyone across society is what the LSO's programs that Clive created were and continue to be about. The media relationships that one develops over a period of time—based on trust, interest and full communication—are essential. He also laid such a solid foundation for his successor, Kathryn McDowell, who has continued this tradition. And Sir Simon Rattle, who is taking over as the LSO's music director in 2017, is enormously involved in all of the LSO Discovery plans and taking music to everyone."

Visceral Connections

Because Carnegie Hall does not have any core artistic partners, it has the luxury of selecting and working with the very best partners across the fields of performance, education and media, and therefore a wealth of informed spokespeople who can share the Hall's vision. Media frequently represents the visceral bridge between events and our ability to experience them, bringing the public world ever closer. How to reconcile the different players? Consumers are looking not only for information but for entertainment; media executives and staff are looking not only for salaries but for career advancement; media shareholders are looking not only for profit but also for influence. And beyond the traditional formats of film and television, magazines and books, radio and newspapers, the ever-expanding social-media channels continue to fracture the public's attention span at home, at work, at school and at the venues themselves, where the perpetual admonition to turn off cellphones—both to prevent ringing and recording—is met with equal parts compliance and defiance.

To be sure, media—when coupled with integrity—offers the hope of increasing social awareness and cultural connections, giving voice to dialogue and diversity as never before. And bylines do not generally start with the kinds of immediate prejudices and preconceptions that personal interactions can still deplorably provoke. As quoted in the UK's *The Guardian* newspaper, author and critic Alex Ross eloquently writes:

> "Blogs written by musicians, singers and people involved behind the scenes... humanise their art form because it has a reputation as being remote and elitist. It's exciting to stress the point that these are living, breathing contemporary people putting on performances with a very complex mix of motives and intellectual impulses. It is not a paper train of robots coming out playing piano and going back to their pod."

Anne-Sophie Mutter's take on the media both observes and challenges:

"We don't seem to have a partner in the media capable of bringing the variation of human creativity to everyone's attention, instead narrowing it down to less and less sophisticated creativity. While people, events and organisations can become commercially successful in certain cases, they often don't really reflect what's happening in society. This can lead to a rather poor understanding of life in general, which makes it easier for radicalism to gain more ground. There are so many colours in between black and white for which one has to develop an understanding. And within politics, it seems that voters often do not care, which is why we get the politicians that we have, those who many times waste their prime position that could otherwise make a difference in the arts. This is one of the reasons why we would hope that the media helps to refocus the lens a little on other subjects rather than just those that are easy to sell."

Media's role will continue to develop, guided by public need, universal expectations for access, the relentless hunger for instant news and reviews, the call for higher standards, and the quest for governmental and societal transparency. Cultural institutions—as much as any competitive business—will need to remain at the forefront of understanding and engaging with this ever-changing field that offers immense opportunities for access, sharing content, engaging with current and potential audiences, creating educational resources, broadening the nature of art and transforming the public's potential for engagement.

In the meantime, one cannot help but smile when considering this contemporary bit of media whimsy: The New York edition of Monopoly has Carnegie Hall as the most valuable site.

19

Maximizing Open Communication

Leaders and staff across a broad range of organizations too often seek to hide behind a veil of confidentiality. Threat versus opportunity: the difference between a heavily guarded culture or one that embraces open communication as an organizational imperative. Gillinson falls into the latter group, believing that almost all information can and should be shared with his team—trustees as well as staff—and that confidentiality between different departments or members of the team should be the exception rather than the norm.

"All too often, the corporate communications function is a dumping ground for tactical managers who are uncomfortable with the quantitative skills needed for success in other functions. But effective communications professionals speak the same language as senior executives and have a deep understanding of the business and its strategy. That often means they have business intuition garnered outside the communications function or from formal education, personal credibility with senior executives, a wide organisational reach, integrity and a strong leadership position in the company. One of the best ways to acquire these attributes is to work at building an informal network of company contacts, getting involved in every aspect of the business. Organisations that continue to take a laissez-faire approach to communications will find it increasingly difficult to compete. Although there will be a continuing need for tactical execution, the addition of an integrated, strategic focus is critical to success. For communications professionals, this imperative will not be a threat but an opportunity: to get a seat at the table and stay there."

Transparency

Jonathan Vaughan makes a telling observation that points to the effectiveness of not always running the gauntlet in one fell swoop:

> "One of the things I always enjoyed watching Clive do at the LSO was to handle difficult decisions for the orchestra through a process of giving information to them over a period of weeks, sometimes months. He would set the landscape and external factors, outlining the issues in a gradual process so that when the big crunch decision was finally taken it usually went through with apparent ease."

What makes people across all organizational levels hesitant to openly share? Is it a matter of feeling like they are losing control or allowing ego to get in the way? Gillinson makes clear that two main motivations likely seduce leaders into becoming secretive, and these are rarely visible to the leaders themselves:

> "The first is seeking power, thinking that by retaining information they will be able to achieve and maintain control. After all, if other people lack the information, it is surely far easier to dominate decision-making. There are two drawbacks to this approach—it doesn't enable them to achieve the best results because they're not getting the benefit of other people's input, and it will ultimately breed mistrust as people will come to understand that they are being manipulated. The second motivation is ego. I remember a head of development I once appointed at the LSO who always wanted every success to be *her* success. Thus she tended to keep her team as well as everyone else at arm's length, and was far less effective than she might have been had she made better use of the excellent people available to her. I made this appointment relatively early on in my days as the LSO's managing director and did not have the experience to read this characteristic at her interview."

Gillinson spoke with her often about this problem, yet she could not or would not bridge that divide. One of the hardest things with such a situation is to help people see themselves as others do. He ultimately had to let her go, as she was unable to hear what he was saying.

> "It is important to acknowledge that you can't see everything at an interview. The more experience you've had, the more questions you

know to ask, the more you can assess someone from an interview, but total insight is impossible. The other major lesson I learned is to take references very seriously, not just in terms of what is said, but almost more importantly, what is not said. It is crucial to appreciate, when checking references, that people generally don't want to say anything overtly damaging about a potential hire, so you have to try to read where the gaps are and test them as much as possible. In my early days as a manager, I was far less aware of when someone giving a reference was not saying something, and I missed signals that I should have picked up. If there's a gap, you've got to be listening to that as much as the words themselves. This is especially true in the United States, because there can be legal implications if you say something negative about someone, even if he or she has been a disaster."

This is where perception enters the room, with the concurrent understanding that all relevant people should be involved in the organization's goals, from hiring to writing a press release. To be sure, self-esteem in the workplace can be both healthy and productive, as it points to self-respect and confidence in one's abilities. Lawyers, for example, having gone to four years of college and three of law school before passing a rigorous bar exam, not only have reason to be confident but in fact must be, given the competition and stakes involved. Doctors require years more training with life and its quality at stake. Executive assistants need to be highly organized and efficient. Insurance salesmen must be well versed in the often-arcane byways of life, home, auto, health and disability. The same parameters of individualized excellence apply to a thousand other professions, which lead to promotions, salary increases, personal fulfillment and positive societal contributions.

Who would anyone rather work with or for, someone who has humility, is inclusive and knows how fortunate he or she is, or someone only concerned about himself or herself? Given how obvious the answer is, it remains astonishing how prevalent—how destructive—the alternative.

In his over three decades in management, Gillinson has worked with many different types of leaders, running the gamut from those he greatly admires, who are always open and collaborative, all the way to total autocrats.

"The tragedy is that there is no way to forge a meaningful or productive relationship with an autocratic leader. No matter how hard you try, how much you use every technique you have ever learned—asking if it would be useful to prepare a fact sheet to enable a productive discussion on a particular issue; offering to pull together the questions that need to be answered in order to make an important decision; suggesting drawing together a group of experts to brainstorm a particular idea; offering to arrange briefing sessions to create context for important decisions—you eventually are forced to accept that these leaders can only hear their own voice, abhor asking questions because they think they already know the answers, and ultimately despise anyone who has the temerity to question their judgment. Since everything for this sort of leader is about themselves and not the mission or the institution, asking questions is not a solution, and they frequently see their own lack of specific knowledge as a virtue. Although I am an eternal optimist, I have found that these are the times in life when you have to move on if you want to remain true to your values and beliefs, however great an apparent opportunity you may be forsaking."

Resources

So many organizations fail to take full advantage of the resources and brainpower that—more often than not—are a mere door away. Gillinson makes clear that every single person at Carnegie Hall knows more about their own job than he does, so if he does not use that knowledge and skill, he is wasting a valuable resource. And by maximizing open communication, never limiting it unless absolutely necessary, corrosive office politics are far less likely to eat away at any culture.

This group dynamic cannot help but enhance fellowship and teamwork—those iconic markers of any healthy organization. If all involved are able—and, to be sure, willing—to see a given challenge as a team effort and not about individual gain or loss, then the job, the achievement, will be elevated to the forefront. As no society is populated by saints, ego will always be present; the key is to manage it in such a way that it can be a positive force.

As a result, Gillinson does not hesitate to raise all key issues with senior staff, regardless of whether potentially divisive or difficult. A culture of trust offers freedom for everyone— including the executive and artistic director— to be able to admit mistakes, and is one of the most liberating tenets of any culture, whether within families, small businesses or the world's top institutions. Peer relationships beyond organizational walls naturally thrive on open communication as well, where trust and confidence buttress the freedom to share, to learn, to grow.

For those organizations that adhere to it, this mindset is recognized not only by colleagues, but inevitably by donors, foundations, customers, the press... really any constituency that interfaces either personally or financially. For a nonprofit, such values tend to stimulate gift-giving and, for a commercial enterprise, they can increase sales. At the same time, board members and executive leadership are privy to sensitive market and competitive data that should remain in-house, which takes nothing away from living by open communication and recognizing that everyone needs to feel involved and part of the discussion, that they have a part to play, that their work is essential.

20

Mission & Objectives
at the Forefront

A visit to most websites of most organizations in most countries reveals an inspiring mission statement. Yet how often is that goal and its associated objectives the primary reason that everyone comes to work? Regardless of an organization's type or breadth, those who persevere with singular focus on their raison d'être are far more likely to thrive.

In one of innumerable inspiring histories, Rupert Scofield—an agricultural economist with two generations of experience in developing countries—cofounded the Foundation for International Community Assistance (FINCA) in 1984, from modest beginnings in microfinance to what is now a global leader with nearly two million clients and a loan portfolio approaching $1 billion. He reflects with a mix of gratitude and advice:

> "If you discover—and I hope everyone does—that thing you care so much about, maybe it's some injustice in the world that really makes you angry and makes you want to do something about it, or some huge international problem like global warming or terrible disease, don't let go of it. That fire is going to keep you going when adversity comes, as it surely will. Especially in the early days when you're trying to promote your idea, you're going to run into skeptic after skeptic and naysayer after naysayer. Just harken back to why you're doing what you're doing. Because we've stuck to our values and mission at FINCA, we've had wonderful things happen and have helped to sustain countless lives along the way."

Carnegie Hall's close adherence to its mission and objectives—continually at the forefront for staff, donors, the media, subscribers, partners and educators—allies it to a growing legion of organizations across our ever-smaller planet that exist to joyfully share their mission, whether that entails offering village banking in Uganda or presenting the world's greatest music and performers in New York City. Despite the man-made barriers that continue to block regions and cultures, positive objectives and outreach help to ensure that the baton is passed from generation to generation. Gillinson's perseverance is as determined as it is tireless:

> "It's vital to ensure that our fundamental values, beliefs and objectives remain part of the conversation with trustees and staff on an ongoing basis. It may be boring for some that our leadership team keeps highlighting these repeatedly, but it's important for us to continually reinforce them with the board and staff so that, as much as possible, they remain at the forefront of everybody's mind and hopefully become second nature. The leaders of Carnegie Hall's individual departments totally understand this and are themselves consistent champions of our vision. We all have to think of ourselves as ambassadors for our mission or, as Slava Rostropovich more colorfully put it, 'We are all soldiers for music.'"

This does not mean that any mission should become locked in stone; it too should be regularly examined and fine-tuned, and adapted if necessary, as Gillinson has repeatedly found.

> "When we set out to develop a new project at Carnegie Hall, we always seek to ensure that we review the ecology around it, not just the project itself. The National Youth Orchestra of the USA is a good example. We started by looking at everything we were doing in the area of training the finest young musicians, including programs like Ensemble Connect and masterclasses. We also did a thorough survey of the overall national landscape for these kinds of talent-development programs, which was a huge help in enabling us to shape the NYO-USA. Once it had been successfully launched and was flourishing, our ongoing evaluation of what we were learning from it led us to create NYO2. This philosophy helps to keep our thinking alive. We're now considering how to develop a project that recognizes and celebrates music teachers, which came out of a meeting with Paul King of the NYC Department of Education. We were talking about the fact that teachers work so hard and are not sufficiently acknowledged, and that most adults, when asked

who inspired them, who changed their life, almost always mention particular teachers. At Carnegie Hall we do a lot of teacher training, but we want to explore if there is more that we can do to celebrate and nurture teachers. These kinds of conversations happen throughout the organisation all the time. However, it's my responsibility, and that of every organisation's leader, to hold the overview of everything we do, day in and day out."

No one but the leader can meaningfully take responsibility for retaining the whole picture all the time. By definition, others have to do the same for their own area of responsibility, but cannot be expected to do so for the entire organization simultaneously.

"On a few occasions I've been shocked, in talking to people who run organisations, when someone says, 'I'm so busy that I don't have enough time to think strategically.' That's a self-fulfilling statement. If a leader doesn't think strategically, he or she will never have the time to think strategically! It is a central part of the job of any leader to make that time, or the organisation will have no direction or clear purpose, and will be vulnerable to opportunist decision-making that has nothing to do with its mission. A bit of money is offered and they adjust their mission to get it, ending up as a conglomerate that means nothing as a whole. Somebody has to maintain a picture of the totality all the time and never stop testing it—a central part of every leader's job."

Shared Strategy

For most organizations, their mission statement typically lives front and center on websites. Carnegie Hall's board is in tune with the Hall's mission and objectives and were centrally involved when revisiting its mission statement about two years after they brought in Gillinson; he felt that it no longer reflected the Hall's fast-developing national and international role and aspirations, especially with education. Everyone became involved in that process—from trustees to staff— to clearly positive effect.

Contemporary music is yet another area that falls within Carnegie Hall's mission. Audiences are often quite drawn to new music presented well, yet so often presenters are inhibited by their fear of putting these pieces on their programs rather than yet another evening of Beethoven or Tchaikovsky. As monumental a masterpiece as Beethoven's 5th Symphony is and will remain, there is also a genuine buzz among audiences and critics alike for the new opera, the new symphony, the new museum show, the new theater production, the new novel.

From the artist's perspective, Anne-Sophie Mutter has seen a very strong audience for contemporary music throughout the world and freely recognizes her own responsibility:

> "Audiences may not be interested in the standard repertoire but they totally go for the new stuff and it's wonderful! Very often the audience is more adventuresome and open-minded than the presenter. That's where artists come in; they need to persuade first the presenter and then the audience. We always need a new and fresh generation of performers to keep the process of presenting contemporary music alive. Carnegie Hall is certainly doing the right thing, and we need more people like Clive who recognize this and push forward."

Carnegie Hall is pursuing a project, as a central part of its 125th-anniversary celebrations, to commission a minimum of 125 new pieces over five years, an unprecedented commitment to new music. The reasoning behind this is to use the anniversary to celebrate the future of music rather than the past, and the project encompasses every sort of music—classical, jazz, world, folk and popular, as well as the Hall's educational mission. In terms of new music, the Hall has a far broader definition of this than solely music by living composers. In addition to the anniversary commissioning project, it is undertaking an ever more extensive exploration of early music, much of it never before performed at the Hall, as well as explorations of rarely heard repertoire in other areas, including the first-ever single-season cycle in the US of Bruckner's nine numbered symphonies. Thus the Hall's ongoing exploration of "new music" is defined by looking forward, backward and sideways in time, pushing the boundaries in every direction and seeking to offer audiences an ever-changing kaleidoscope of inspiring, challenging and fulfilling journeys of discovery.

And as each generation continues to discover, every day brings its challenges, its rush just to keep up, yet those able to look beyond the daily imperatives of their job give voice to a mission statement that brings the words of a website or annual report to life. Better to speak of it.

21
Soft Power versus Hard Power

Soft power—getting others to want the outcomes that you are seeking—engages rather than coerces. In many areas of life, people question the validity of soft power, often because it is much more complex to plan, enunciate and implement; it rarely involves simple solutions in favor of longer-term thinking. Joseph Nye, Jr.—Harvard University Distinguished Service Professor and former dean of the John F. Kennedy School of Government, with a prominent career as one of America's foreign-policy experts including key United States government posts throughout his vital career—coined the term "soft power" in his 1990 book, *Bound to Lead,* that challenged the then-prevailing perception of America's power decline. He spoke of obtaining results "through attraction and persuasion rather than coercion and payment."

As Nye observes:

> "It's all about appearing macho and tough, and this cowboy-western frontier approach that dominates. A former congresswoman, a great advocate of soft power, said to me, 'I can't get up on my stump to my constituency in California and talk about spending money on soft power—I just wouldn't get elected! But if I say that we should spend more on our defense budget, I will get elected.' On the other hand, we look at a country like Britain, where the British Academy recently had a study of soft power in the House of Lords, and referred to it frequently."

The American scene plays into this, as demonstrated only too clearly in the 2016 US presidential election race. Some candidates have deliberately set out to feed fear in order to validate simplistic hard-power solutions. Yet ironically, many people who spend time thinking about soft power are in the military. When discussing counterinsurgency, as just one of many issues, winning hearts and minds is a central weapon, as Nye has seen firsthand:

"Those in the Pentagon who plan for heavy counter-violent extremism always make a place for soft power. People in operational situations pay quite a bit of attention to soft power. Politicians who have to get elected, on the other hand, have to appeal to the general public, which suffers partly from media and cultural traditions putting forth that 'softness' doesn't pay."

Joseph Nye

There is an understanding among many, both within and outside of government and the military, that ISIS cannot be defeated solely by bombs and bullets, and a way must be found to alter the narrative. However, it is far more challenging to win over hearts and minds to this more sophisticated and long-term approach, rather than to simplistic proposals that purport to offer the chance to wipe out that which we fear.

Is there, then, a way to break through such a barrier to reach the general public? Nye recognizes how much harder that is, because in the public debate, people want to get elected and the electorate wants its officials to appear tough, with clear sound-bite answers. Talking big and ruthless is so much easier, appealing as it does to people's desire for straightforward solutions; soft power is by definition far more complex and much harder to enunciate in a compelling way. In addition, hard power will always seek to personify soft power as weak. "Listen to how hard Donald Trump works," Nye observes, "to give the impression that he's tougher than anyone else! Or Ted Cruz, who has talked about carpet-bombing Syria and ISIS until 'the sand glows in the dark' as if this will solve every problem."

Attracting People and Resources

Beyond the political sphere, there is a widespread understanding of soft power in business; much advertising and brand loyalty reflect this. Nonprofits also rely heavily on it. The larger ones do have some economic power because of the scale of their budgets, but the ability to attract people to support them—including financial—is essential, and soft power is central to this. Engaging and attracting others is crucial, whether in business, government, NGOs, nonprofits or hospitals; the appeal of organizations that practice soft power tends to be on many levels, some of it subliminal. In terms of employees, creating a culture that attracts and sustains relationships and commitment is crucial to most people's enjoyment of their jobs and lives, and tangibly pays off.

Soft power can also be effective in negotiations of all types. When it comes down to making final accommodations to reach the best possible agreement, how each side feels about the other often makes a difference. Nye shares this truism with a smile: "Hating their guts will almost always lead to less flexibility!" As a tactic, calculated anger and bluster are among any number of approaches that are used and, while such gambits can be successful some of the time, they often backfire. Equally, if soft power ever gives the impression that it represents weakness, then it also will fail.

In his 2015 report for the Getty Museum, Nye makes clear an effective approach that applies equally well to a wide range of organizations:

> "In the long term, there will always be elements of both competition and cooperation in international relationships, but countries have more to gain from the cooperative element, which can be strengthened by the rise of mutual soft power. Moreover, we are all enriched as we present attractive cultures to each other. Smart policies should aim to make that a trend in this century."

Part of effective persuasion means having a strong position to begin with, without which it is hard to project credible confidence; this can rarely be faked between tough negotiators. It also requires genuine conviction and strength, and an ability to communicate these, since those who practice hard power often fall into the trap of mistaking soft power for weakness.

Those who get what they want through intimidation and fear rather than collaboration continue to persist. Business textbooks are littered with stories such as that of "Chainsaw Al" Dunlap, whose ruthless techniques at Sunbeam, for example, drove it to bankruptcy. We live in a world that is often dominated by short-term thinking; soft power is a subtler, often more lasting approach, and therefore harder to defend in relation to short-term battles. There is, however, an increasing recognition of the effectiveness of soft power among management and leadership. Nye's book *The Powers to Lead* offers key examples in business, the military and other areas that show soft power becoming more prevalent and recognized in an information world.

In one of innumerable cultural examples, soft power has been extremely effective at The Philadelphia Orchestra, which emerged from bankruptcy and brought in the dynamic young conductor Yannick Nézet-Séguin, who is naturally collaborative and inclusive. Not only are these impactful qualities, but the employees—in this case musicians and staff—truly like and respect him. Musical decisions ultimately rest with him, but the musicians feel involved and instinctively respond to his leadership, as does the city of Philadelphia.

Society as a whole appears to be embracing soft power more than in the past, but the political atmosphere remains largely stuck. Much of America's soft power is generated by civil society, from entertainment to universities to foundations, rather than by its political leaders. A successful soft-power strategy must be seen as legitimate in the eyes of others. As Nye reminds us, President Dwight Eisenhower once noted that leadership is the ability to get people to work together, not only because you tell them to do so and enforce your orders, but because they instinctively want to do it for you.

A More Lasting Approach

When Gillinson started managing the LSO, the dangerous situation in which the orchestra found itself required radical solutions that he did not have the power to impose; the LSO is owned by the players, so the managing director ultimately reports to them. Although he had the counterbalancing benefit of the players being well aware of the fact that without drastic changes the orchestra may well cease to exist, there was nonetheless strong resistance from many players to a number of his proposed changes. The major asset that he had was that, as a player in the orchestra for 14 years, he knew and understood the players' psychology as one of them. He therefore knew that the only way to address resistance to change was through persuasion; in the long run, an unwavering commitment to values and meaningful objectives would succeed, and nothing important would be achieved except by taking the players with him on that journey. It was not about winning, but of prevailing for the larger good, and this philosophy had to grow out of meaningful values related to the purpose of the LSO's existence.

"I soon discovered how badly people can behave when they perceive their own self-interest to be at stake. More broadly, there will always be situations in life where, in order to get what they want, people will act ruthlessly and you never achieve anything important by behaving badly because others do. In the end, if you allow others to undermine or even destroy your values, you will have diminished yourself and be the long-term loser. In addition, following others down the path of ruthlessness and destruction of values is highly unlikely to lead to meaningful outcomes, even if you 'win' one or two battles. That said, it is very important to understand that there is a difference between being tough and being aggressive or destructive. To be effective in management, one has to be tough and—depending on circumstances—implacably strong, but that is not the same as ruthless. Strength is incredibly important, but remaining true to your own values needs to permeate every aspect of life."

As Gillinson reflects:

"When I first went into management, I was often defensive because I felt totally insecure about my own ability to do the job (for good reason!) and would respond quite aggressively to what I saw as questions about my leadership. That was something I had to learn, which frankly took me a long time. That is why having people around whom we trust, and who will always tell us the difficult things we need to hear, is so important. It can be very difficult to accept personal criticism, but if we reach the stage when we no longer seek nor hear it, then we are the losers and will almost certainly have stopped growing as human beings. The challenge with so much in life is that most things are progressive. Even though the pace of change may be imperceptible, by the end of the journey the change can be immense, like evolution on a condensed timescale."

The progressive nature of both learning and behavior is clear:

"You may think that one small unethical act does not matter, is invisible, and was in any case necessary; the end justified the means. However, by making it, the next one will have become easier and the one after that easier still. Once you have started down that path, the chances are that you will continue down it, with ever-decreasing concerns about doing so. Similarly, the use and effectiveness of soft power is also progressive, and most people have to learn how to use it. I certainly had to. It's neither an easy nor always an obvious route—after all, if attacked, the instinct is to hit back! An eye for an eye. It takes a lot of training and awareness not to react out of emotion, but instead out of fundamental values and beliefs."

Leaders and managers brought in to overcome entrenched, often stubborn cultures—as happened to Gillinson at the LSO—almost always find the process of change difficult. Ultimately, the task at hand is to engage people with a vision that gives them hope and a sense of possibility, a belief that things can be better and more exciting, ultimately leading to a more fulfilling life. Gillinson echoes a widespread perception:

"Looking again at the 2016 US presidential election, too many of the campaigns have been based on seeking to generate fear and anger: the country's getting worse, fear of terrorism, barely concealed racism, other countries are exploiting us; overall, everything that we're unhappy or concerned about is somebody else's fault and if we could only hit out at them everything would be fine. These tactics are all based on appealing to lowest-common-denominator instincts. One of the biggest challenges for politics worldwide right now is that people feel so let down by politicians that even if they do enunciate messages of hope, it is not clear that anyone will believe them anymore. Running an arts organisation has to be about aspiration and inspiration, of how we make life better for others. Carnegie Hall *engages* people with music so that it enhances their lives. In the end, if we do that really well, we will unquestionably have looked after the Hall as well. At the beginning of my journey at the LSO, positive outcomes for the players could not be demonstrated in advance, which is why the power of persuasion was vital. Part of our job was to inspire enough people with a mission and direction they could feel passionate about, and through this create the momentum that would enable us to enact change. There was no way we would succeed unless enough players believed in the values and objectives."

There is little difference among nonprofits, businesses and other organizational structures in how they benefit from soft power. Marquee companies like Facebook and Google, with seemingly endless power and money at their fingertips, recognize that any attempt to exercise hard power would damage their brands irreparably. They succeed through the power of ideas and imagination, and through understanding and serving people's needs. A company such as Starbucks receives goodwill from its staff—and, by extension, its customers—by fully paying the college-education tuitions of its employees through an innovative College Achievement Plan in collaboration with Arizona State University. Domineering bosses may well force high levels of service for a limited time, yet the genuine desire to serve—fostered by soft power—cannot be faked. Within both for-profits and nonprofits, domineering board members are likewise becoming more of a minority as time goes by. It is fascinating to explore the value of soft power to the US State Department, which is very clear about the immense long-term value of the NYO-USA in terms of building relationships worldwide, especially in countries where standard diplomacy is struggling.

Given the repeatedly proven effectiveness of soft power to encourage awareness, insight and access, it is surprising that it is not more widely embraced, yet many so-called highly successful public figures—from billionaires on down—say, "The reason I'm successful is because I'm ruthless and can always be tougher than the other guy." However, one of the encouraging signs of our times is that this sort of leader is becoming less common, with ever more leaders seeking to be inclusive team-builders.

Oscar Wilde's characteristically succinct observation is an ironically apposite tribute to hard power: "Some cause happiness wherever they go; others whenever they go."

Difficulties Notwithstanding

Gillinson makes clear that soft power is generally much more complicated to implement than hard power, which tends to be relatively straightforward:

> "Practitioners of hard power broadly define their task in simple terms: You just need to be tougher than the next guy and able to crush all opposition. Soft power is not only far more complex, it can also be very difficult to sustain, particularly when faced by those who

seek to use brute force to prevail. It is far from reflexive, since hard power is much easier to sell in terms of our survival instincts. Those who practice soft power understand that in most cases it is more powerful than hard power when used with courage and commitment. However, it cannot be abandoned halfway through a given project or relationship just because the situation becomes difficult, and the level of self-restraint it demands can be almost painful at times."

Hard power takes many forms. Limitless car collisions—let alone the wide range of darker human behavior—happen because drivers cannot seem to step back. They *have* to get even with that guy. They *have* to knock him off. They *have* to get ahead. The results can be as tragic as they are unnecessary. Gillinson is realistic:

"Human nature makes a real mixture of us all. We're just as much ruthless animals—programmed to kill rather than be killed—as we are social animals who need to work together to survive, sometimes making personal sacrifices for the good of the tribe. Soft power often means watching other people demonstrate all of their anger and aggression, and having to absorb it in order to enable them to move on. It can be a tough and lonely experience."

D.H. Lawrence once said that the ideal man is a first-rate thinker and a first-rate animal. Gillinson's response?

"Clearly, there are times when soft power no longer has any meaning. Jews caught up in Hitler's final solution were trapped in a situation where there was no conscience, no morality, no values, and law and order had disappeared as far as their fate was concerned. Soft power has no meaning in such a context. When the world is faced by a Hitler, I reluctantly accept that hard power is the only answer, and in such circumstances I find it impossible to accept that conscientious objection is a meaningful posture."

If people are not willing to fight to sustain core beliefs, integrity means nothing. Gillinson has carefully considered the issue.

"I have no doubt that soft power is the right answer virtually all of the time. However, it is also important to be able to judge when it isn't, and I have been fortunate enough never to have been in such a situation. Whatever reservations anyone might have about the society we live in, it has laws and values that, if lived by, almost always give us some protection regardless of the most impossibly destructive situations or people we might have to face. But when the rules disappear, soft power almost certainly won't win, one of the reasons why Nelson Mandela was so extraordinary. Despite a regime that was ruthless in so many ways, and placed almost no value on black lives, he understood that they nonetheless retained some vestiges of humanity, and he risked his life on that bet. Amazingly he was right and managed to touch the humanity in them. However, if the South African government had been led by a Hitler, they'd have killed Mandela without a second thought. His achievement was not just to use soft power to defeat apartheid, an historic achievement of itself, but to use it again, through his extraordinary spirit of forgiveness, to bring whites, blacks and others together as the rainbow nation, in a way that no one would have believed possible in advance. What he did was superhuman, and to me he's the greatest man of our age. His was the ultimate demonstration of what can be achieved through soft power that could never have been accomplished in any other way."

22
Being Your Own Toughest Critic

One of Boulez's favorite sayings was that being an artist is like riding a bicycle; if you don't keep moving forward, you fall off. This applies to a broad range of professions and pursuits, and being self-critical is a necessary mindset for lifelong learning and growth. The key is to use self-criticism as a positive and motivating force, rather than one that leads to feelings of disappointment, frustration, guilt, anger, anxiety or even self-pity. Negativity can be paralyzing. Self-awareness and being tough on oneself, when used positively, can act as the most constructive and energizing of catalysts, enabling people to keep progressing throughout life.

In Gillinson's case, he was always analytical, not only about external things, but also about feelings and thoughts.

"As a boy, my father used to tell me that I overanalyzed everything, but I have come to accept that is who I am. In my early years it grew out of insecurity, but is now part of challenging myself and goes hand in hand with never being satisfied. I don't think that we should ever see any achievement as 'Great, it's done.' What matters is 'What's next?' and 'What has our current achievement enabled us to do in the future?' Yes, it was wonderful when the NYO-USA stepped onto the platform and performed their first fabulous concert; we were thrilled with what had been achieved, but no sooner was the project flying than we began to ask ourselves: 'What have we learned from this? How can we make it better? What else should we do to nurture the finest talent?' I cannot remember a time when I was satisfied with the status quo, and at Carnegie Hall we try to ensure that we are never satisfied with standing still. We must never stop asking how tomorrow can be even better than today."

Constantly seeking to improve is one of the most enduring values for creative people. Gillinson will always remember how impatient Rostropovich was with flattery at the end of a concert:

> "He was his own greatest critic and always knew what he could do better. After a performance his mind had already moved on to what he wanted to work on the next time he played that piece of music. I vividly remember when he told me that he thought at last the time had come to record the Bach cello suites, which he and most cellists consider the ultimate pinnacle of the cello repertoire. Early in his life he had decided that he would not record them until he felt he was ready, and then only under very specific conditions. His recording company had been asking him to record the suites for almost as long as he could remember, but his answer had always been 'I am not ready yet.' At last, in his 60s, he decided that he wanted to do this, but totally at his own expense, so that if he was not satisfied with the recording, he could destroy it. He spent a lot of time seeking a church with the right acoustics, and when in the end he found what he was looking for, in France, he spent days there, with a hand-picked recording team whom he paid personally, playing the suites over and over again until he had captured the performances in which he could believe. At last his company had their long-coveted recording. Even after all of that, there is no doubt that he continued to think about and develop his interpretations of the Bach suites. This is one of the defining characteristics that I value in the people I have come to treasure and admire throughout my life, be it friends, great artists, the extraordinary teams I've worked with at the LSO and Carnegie Hall, or the remarkable trustees and supporters. Never being satisfied and continually seeking to move forward is where the artist resides in the life of every human being. It ties in with what I think is the most important talent for any artist, underpinning every other: humility. If ever this gets lost, their journey as an artist is over."

One of the challenges that leaders face is the higher they move up the ladder, the less people are willing to criticize or question their judgment. Gillinson and many other leaders try to push their senior teams to tell them whenever they think they are making a mistake or mishandling something, yet employees do not find this easy, even if asked. It is vital for leaders to identify people whom they trust, who will say the difficult things to them, and who also trust their leader enough to know that if criticized it will not be to their detriment. The last thing that anyone wants is to have a discussion, come to an artificial agreement and implement a flawed plan or project, only to discover that many people did not think it a good idea and did not want to speak up. It is equally important to know that, if you express your concern to a leader about something that he or she has done, your candidness will be valued and not punished.

In his early days managing the LSO, Gillinson was in such a hurry to get so much done that he often pushed too hard, trying to bulldoze his ideas through. He quickly learned that by doing so and then having to pull back, it took even longer to get the decision he sought than had he given people sufficient time to assimilate the new ideas in the first place. He learned that timing was as important a skill as developing great ideas. At the start he knew little about leadership, never having been in such a position before, and fully accepts that there were many things he got wrong and did not know. He was forced to learn quickly.

Leading by Example

To engender both goodwill and the genuine desire to serve among employees, leading by example is essential. Enlightened CEOs want to make sure their staff knows—truly understands—that he or she is open to criticism. In fact, leaders who do not require constant ego-petting generally enjoy being challenged. Of course, cultural norms continue to prevail, as Gillinson quickly discovered:

> "On arriving at Carnegie Hall, I found that Americans are more respectful of seniority than the British. It was much easier for somebody at the LSO to say to me, 'Look Clive, I don't agree with you. I think you're talking rubbish.' We'd then discuss it. Here in the US, for whatever reason, people seem to defer more to authority and have an expectation that leaders will be more autocratic. It took a while to create a truly collaborative culture, to ensure that Carnegie Hall's senior team understood that I thought the only way to arrive at the best decisions was to use our joint expertise."

The idea of anyone being perfect all the time is absurd. Why, then, is it so hard for some people to acknowledge imperfections, to ask for help and apologize when appropriate, to move on without pretense? This is a clear reflection of insecurity, as Gillinson experienced:

"Because I was very insecure in my early days in management, that made it difficult for me to acknowledge when I got something wrong and to learn from people; my instinctive reaction was always to push back. People's inability to accept criticism or acknowledge they've made a mistake is usually rooted in insecurity or arrogance, which often go together."

The inability to get beyond acknowledging mistakes often prevents people from moving forward quickly. Gillinson tries to ensure that his staff is comfortable telling him if they have made a mistake or have a problem, and that he is always available to work with them on the solution.

"I always set out to build relationships of mutual trust whereby members of my team will come to me if there's a problem we need to discuss; it is then possible to delegate extensively and give them a lot of space. However, if a problem arises and I only hear about it once it has become bigger, that trust will be undermined and it will become necessary to reduce the autonomous space in which that person works."

Promoting such a culture of encouraging staff to be forthright, open about problems or mistakes, and freely coming to management is far from the environment of fear that inevitably develops from autocracy. This was a facet of Sanford Weill's chairmanship of Carnegie Hall that Gillinson valued enormously over the 10-plus years they worked together. Weill's central mantra of delegation was that he never wanted surprises. He would always be there to discuss problems with Gillinson when asked, but gave him extensive autonomy based on being kept fully up to date on everything that was going on, allied to the fact that Gillinson would always raise concerns or problems as soon as he became aware of them.

"In America, more than anywhere I know, people tend to think that leadership is above all about being strong and decisive, and leaders are more likely to be put on a pedestal. In the corporate world this tends to go hand in hand with huge salaries and a perception that the success of a company is about the leader rather than the team. This is also reflected in earnings differentials, where the difference between the people at the top and the bottom of a company is extreme. There is an admiration for power, for firm leadership, so it requires a greater effort to create an inclusive and engaged culture."

People working under autocratic leaders are constantly in fear—of destructive and counterproductive criticism, of being fired, of demotion or more generally of erratic decisions. This is likely to lead to a fear of taking risks, thus reducing creativity.

"I've dealt with financially successful business leaders who are autocrats and it's a huge challenge, because all too often they think they know everything, that everything is about answers, and that they have all the answers! They make assumptions about the transferability of knowledge from one business to another that are frequently meaningless, and yet their supreme belief in themselves precludes them from asking questions rather than giving answers, thus leading to fundamentally flawed decision-making. Without an exchange of ideas, without asking questions, without using the people resources of a company, the chances of making good decisions are small. It is wasteful in every way and creates a lot of ill will—a very demoralising environment in which to work, whether in a for-profit or nonprofit organisation."

Anne-Sophie Mutter, in common with so many extraordinary artists and, in fact, with broad-minded people of every career, well recognizes the necessity of being tough on herself:

"Humility is so crucial; who are we compared to the composer? Self-doubt is so necessary and artists have to put question marks behind what they're doing. That is why I find it very important to step back from what I'm doing from time to time—a week, a month or even longer—to really evaluate if what's been done in the past few years is good enough, if there is any sign of falling into habit, which is a deadly poison in relationships as well as in the life of an artist. One has to be very attentive to routine, which is like a great blanket covering everything—the ultimate killer in life."

23

Never Allowing Yourself to Be Defined by Others

Gillinson's realization that we should never be defined by other people's behavior—and if others behave badly, we should nonetheless behave well— came at an early point in his life, by reading biographies and becoming aware of figures like Gandhi and Mandela. He came to understand from the lives of such people the importance of always retaining one's own values. Literature and being self-analytical were catalysts for learning, but initially Gillinson absorbed this subliminally more than rationally:

> "It's not a question of trying to be a saint, which is way beyond almost anyone's wildest dreams, even if anyone wanted to become one—and I'm sure that most people don't! It's the realisation that if people behave ruthlessly, we can damage ourselves irreparably if we respond by abandoning our own values in order to fight them on their terms. Ironically, this sort of person is far more confused by people who behave well than by those who match them weapon for weapon. If people are not inhibited by a value system, and you try to fight them on their own terms, they will almost certainly win; they are professionals in this arena. What makes things even worse is that they'll win twice over, not just the battle, but also by destroying your values and changing who you are. Such issues have been faced by people, companies and countries in every place and at every time."

Learning from rather than being defined by other people—whether peers, staff, friends or family—occupies an entirely different, positive realm. One must not, however, be negatively swayed by difficulties, nor respond to them with ethical shortcuts. When someone behaves badly, the natural temptation is to want to damage him or her, which is often not hard to do. This harks back to how much more effective and powerful soft power is than hard power.

Such awareness represents an often far-from-smooth process of defining oneself, which can easily go against the grain of instinctive human behavior. Gillinson found the early search for self-knowledge fascinating, if not particularly enjoyable:

> "Self-analysis and endless introspection may offer a meaningful amount of self-knowledge, but as far as I was concerned, they did not offer a productive path towards happiness. The fundamental problem was that putting myself at the center of my own universe was not fulfilling, whatever self-help books might suggest; in fact, focussing on oneself is to me a fundamental flaw of so many such books. The first time I really started enjoying life was when it stopped being about me and became about working for an institution that could make a difference to others."

An Ongoing Process

Some people say (and often with good reason!) that none of us ever change; we are who we are. Gillinson does not subscribe to this thinking, although accepting that some fundamentals remain a lifelong part of who we are.

> "We do, or should, keep growing and developing throughout our lives, trying to do things better than we did them yesterday, trying to understand and learn more, treat people better, contribute more to their lives. I was shocked when I went back to a school reunion recently. By being thrown together with so many of the people I grew up with, all the feelings that had defined my life at that time came rushing back, and made me acutely aware that I bore little resemblance to the person they had all known then, and I guess who they all thought they knew still."

Anne-Sophie Mutter stresses the need to take time to find one's place, which equally applies to the most fulfilling careers:

> "It can be a question of how secure a person feels with what he or she wants to pursue. I had wonderful tutoring and experiences with Herbert von Karajan when I was young, but it was a different time

then. Today, the media and the need to be an instant success is quite a burden. Developing repertoire slowly—and trusting the hope that quality will prevail—really does matter, yet there's no simple recipe. We all have different temperaments and temperatures and speeds in life; some will appear very quickly, have a great ride and then perhaps disappear. Struggle definitely helps to build character and perseverance. And it's totally normal to struggle, to have failed.... Why is that so hard to accept? It's reality! One has to forgive oneself as long as the true effort has been given. Picking oneself up, knowing that improvement will happen, is key."

Multitalented people at the very highest level, both on the cusp of careers or well into their professional lives, can broadly go one of two ways: Like Busoni and Rachmaninov, and one of the most remarkable polymaths of all, Leonard Bernstein, they can proceed regardless of the public's and critics' unwillingness to accept that they can be extraordinary in more ways than one, or they find it confusing and narrow their horizons. In Rachmaninov's words,

"The musicians and critics were always waiting to devour me. One would say: Rachmaninov is not a composer, but a pianist. And another: He is primarily a conductor. But the public... I love it. Everywhere and at all times it has treated me wonderfully."

Gillinson shares a telling story of Rostropovich about what lasts regardless of what others would have happen:

"In 1990 Slava returned to Moscow with the National Symphony Orchestra, of which he was then its music director, for his first visit back since leaving the Soviet Union in 1974. At the time he and his wife left, soon after which they had their citizenship withdrawn, he thought he would never again be allowed to return to his country. I was thrilled to be invited by him as one of his guests on the trip, and his homecoming was a huge success. One of the most memorable and moving moments occurred when the whole orchestra and guests were invited to the Moscow State Circus. Slava was going to be a little late—he told me later that he was visiting the graves of Shostakovich and Prokofiev—but when he arrived the circus master came into the ring and stopped the circus in order to welcome him. The place exploded with applause and cheers. It was almost impossible to comprehend that for over 16 years he had been written out of every history book, his name had disappeared from every public place or communication, his recordings had been suppressed or destroyed, and yet here he was, back after all those years and somehow every person in that audience knew who he was—a man who supposedly did not exist!"

Gillinson tells of another cellist who would not be defined by others, despite great personal struggle:

"Douglas (Dougie) Cummings was one of the greatest British cello talents and a totally natural, brilliant and expressive player. At the time of his appointment, he was the youngest-ever principal cellist in the LSO's history. After he had a stroke, he managed to pull his playing back together, but it was never quite the same, and little by little it became less reliable. In the end, the LSO board decided that his playing was no longer consistent enough for this position, and discussed how to address this with him. Because he had brought me into the orchestra as a cellist, they decided that I was the right person to talk to him (by this time I was managing the orchestra), even though performance issues were normally handled player to player. Our view was that he needed to have counselling of some sort, to ensure that he acknowledged what the problems were with his playing, and he also needed time off to practice. I asked one of our donors to fund his time off and, once I had raised the money, met with Dougie. It was probably the hardest and most emotional meeting of my life at the LSO and by its end I was the one totally shaken up. He was completely in control and said that he had an upcoming tour of Australia with a chamber group and would get back to me afterwards. His decision, although it was hard to leave the LSO and he greatly appreciated the offer, was that he would much rather be a big fish in a small pond than undertake an uncertain struggle to get his playing back to the highest level. Because his whole personality and life had been about a passion for and love of life and music, always carried effortlessly to the top by his remarkable talent, fighting to regain that mountaintop was not how he wanted to spend his time. He understood his own personality and undoubtedly made the right decision."

Unequivocal Messages

Gillinson once asked Boulez about the fact that he seemed to have become so much calmer and perhaps less of a revolutionary as he had grown older, unwilling to fit into predetermined or expected molds. He replied, "When a river is young, at the top of the mountain, it's fiery, splashy and very noisy. However, when it gets to the bottom of the mountain and is more mature, it looks much more peaceful but it is much more powerful."

Jonathan Vaughan has seen firsthand how Gillinson and people like him define themselves—unequivocal about who they are, what they do and why they do it, a process that naturally translates into any organization having the courage to define itself.

> "This isn't just lip service to introduce a strategic plan, but an ongoing, rigorous and effortful process. Defining oneself has often challenged orthodox views both inside and outside of organisations and frequently sets up a platform for intensive debate. But in the end, the organisation is invariably much stronger for understanding its own purpose, while the naysayers and well-poisoners have either come on board or left. The result is an absolutely crystal-clear message to the outside world."

24

Continual Self-Improvement & Lifelong Learning

Why is it that some people turn to a musical instrument or a foreign language or college courses or continually challenging work to keep their minds active, while others essentially stop learning at age 40 or even earlier?

Ian Martin has witnessed this throughout his career:

> "I've seen many people move through organisations to the point at which they're not fit to be promoted further, as they're struggling with their current job. In the investment banking industry, for example, in which I worked, people became so sure of themselves; they had been promoted and felt they could almost walk on water, that they knew everything, and really stopped learning and growing. In many industries it's a dog-eat-dog competitive world, and the last thing one can do is to show humility or uncertainty, pretending to know things when that's not the case. The best managers and leaders are those who continually iterate what they're doing and surround themselves with people who can help them make informed decisions and move forward."

Carnegie Hall—among a broad range of for-profit, nonprofit and community organizations—is all about developing curiosity and exploration, about offering new challenges. The citywide international festivals that the Hall has presented since 2007 offer people the opportunity to explore beyond their normal boundaries, be they classical music, theater, film, dance or other cultural pursuits. Many people are not omnivores in terms of learning, yet what joys lie in the sense of discovery!

Gillinson elaborates:

"What we try to do with our festivals is to tempt people to explore outside their comfort zone. After all, if you love music you may be interested to explore the visual arts or theater or dance, but unless you have some knowledge or experience, you won't necessarily know how or where to start—the choice is confusing and often overwhelming, which can result in making no choices. You may come to Carnegie Hall because you love African-American music, or the music of South Africa or Venice or China or Vienna or Latin America or Leonard Bernstein or Japan, but through our festivals we hope that you will be tempted by other aspects of these cultures, provided by trusted curators that include many of the city's greatest cultural institutions like MoMA, the Met Museum, Guggenheim Museum, Apollo Theater, City Center and the New York Public Library, amongst many others. This radically reduces the perceived risk of experimenting, while actively encouraging people to explore in ways they might otherwise never do."

In just one of countless examples, both within and beyond the arts, The Philadelphia Orchestra's program guides some years ago started adding context when writing about the music to be performed. What was the concurrent literature? What was happening in society at the time? Subscribers and guests alike gratefully respond to such presentations. Gillinson likewise sees part of Carnegie Hall's job as to stimulate and give people the opportunity to engage in fascinating journeys. As a result, audience numbers for the participating partners have expanded well beyond what they would have been had they presented the same events without the festival context: a transforming experience for most of those involved.

In addition to the positive impact on many thousands of people, this mindset applies when looking inward as well, toward the organization's entire staff. In common with enlightened organizations worldwide, Carnegie Hall's senior-staff agenda includes nurturing those who work for them and adding to their skills. This may equip them for promotions or, frankly, to change employers. While perhaps a risk, the approach of investing in people is crucial, with the resulting skills and goodwill creating, on balance, clearly productive outcomes.

Joseph Polisi echoes an intrinsic belief shared by many of his colleagues across cities, across institutions, across age groups: "It is our role, at places like Juilliard and Carnegie Hall, to provide the resources for lifelong learners to participate, especially now with distance learning, with apps, with digital opportunities that make it much more accessible and can also keep the mind vibrant into old age."

While harder for smaller organizations to offer this kind of support, largely a matter of limited resources, they can and do nonetheless encourage self-improvement. As there is no downside to such pursuits, why are they not more actively embraced across the board?

Curiosity

Gillinson returns to this theme:

> "If people are always curious and wanting to grow, then self-improvement is the byproduct. There's always the temptation to pursue the result rather than the stimulus. Being fascinated by learning new things—the exploration—is what actually matters, as when people say it's the journey that counts, not the destination. And besides, will there ever be a destination?"

Given every possible upside to continual learning, is it a matter of laziness when not pursued? Is it ego among those who feel that they have arrived?

> "I'm sure there are many answers, including that if people have been brought up without questions around them or anybody nurturing their curiosity, it is likely to have been stifled; after all, almost every child has innate curiosity, yet many adults do not. Another part could be about education, too much of which is still linear with right or wrong answers, which does not engage a child's imagination. And if parents have little imagination and don't think in terms of personal development, they likely won't pass these values on to their children. I also think that for several generations television has played a part: Children and adults have spent far too much of their lives in passive consumption. To me, a meaningful hope for the future is that so much of the new-media world involves interaction and participation, so this could—and hopefully will—have a transformational impact on engaging imagination and creativity in many different ways."

Parental reach can be difficult given ever-more-hectic schedules and, increasingly, both parents working. The Weill Music Institute does try to involve them, yet would do far less work with children were they having to concurrently engage parents. Among WMI's goals is to provide the spark and stimulus to children so that they want—in fact, are eager—to learn more. And if they then share that with their parents, all the better.

Age is not a barrier to accessing that spark. As a child, Gillinson always wanted to create things and, at age 70, he is ever more eager to learn and grow, finding life more exciting and interesting than ever before. Within his circle, this is not unusual, but the caveat is both revealing and common:

> "People tend to like and know and have friends who share similar tastes, values and interests. Some get comfortable—with jobs, friends, family. I don't enjoy being comfortable with anything with which I'm engaged, and I rarely get exhausted when working flat out; the one thing that tires me is boredom. Being excited, involved and engaged stimulates energy. When I'm interviewing potential new staff members or listening to a performance—whether in a concert hall, for an audition or as a competition judge—the biggest single giveaway is if I start to yawn. Whatever else I may be telling myself— that they're really interesting, intelligent or whatever—I have learned to heed that signal. At the 2015 Tchaikovsky competition, when the ultimate winner of the cello prize—Andrei Ioniță—played, he commanded everyone's attention from the very first note. Everyone was sitting differently. Attentive. It's amazing how the body transmits all of this unconsciously. Even if people know nothing about music, when listening to a compelling artist, their attention is engaged. We often try to kid ourselves: If we *think* we're going to something good or important, we'll try to convince ourselves of that and applaud the reputation rather than what we are hearing from the stage. Our assumption is often that it's great because we 'know' it's great."

Preconceptions and expected norms continue to pervade all aspects of relationships, whether personal or professional, and they can vary enormously from country to country. When Gillinson started at Carnegie Hall, he wanted to invite each of the senior staff team out for lunch separately, to start getting to know them in a more informal environment than the office, yet…

> "The next thing I knew, the place was in a panic because all the senior staff thought that, because I was a Brit, I was inviting them out to lunch to tell them politely that they had gotten the sack, rather than just sacking them directly like a new American manager

might have done! Thereafter I decided that I'd better find a cultural translator and, having met with a number of key arts leaders, Glenn Lowry became not only a good friend, but a terrific sounding board for things where I wasn't sure if my understanding of our common language was the same as the people I was working with!"

Lowry observes a trait common to most artists, yet surely not to be taken for granted among managers:

"Clive began his career as a professional cellist, and one cannot be an artist without a burning desire to be better all the time, to hone the craft, to look for how to be that much better than the day before. All of that is woven into the way he approaches running Carnegie Hall. He's not satisfied to come in and see that it's running well, but how to make it better, what's the next project, how to expand the reach, how to build a youth orchestra.... All of these initiatives grow out of a kind of restlessness to push himself and the institution to another level."

When reflecting on the institution, Gillinson continues to marvel at the Hall's creation—a magical piece of history unique in the world—and how its architect, barely in his mid-30s and a gifted amateur cellist, implemented what he learned.

"Andrew Carnegie's wife sang in the Oratorio Society of New York and, as there was no good concert hall in New York at that time, she asked her husband to build one (as one does!). Andrew Carnegie did not seek out the leading architect of the day, or someone who had already built a concert hall, but instead he engaged a good—though not top—architect, William Tuthill, who was the Oratorio Society's treasurer. Carnegie then sent him around Europe to study all the best concert halls and he came back and designed Carnegie Hall, which bore no relationship to anything he had seen. If you ask acousticians about the fundamentals that define the best concert halls, they mostly say shoebox shaped, approximately 2,000 seats, no curves. Carnegie Hall has 2,800 seats with curves front and back and is definitely not shaped like any shoebox I have ever seen. Nonetheless, Tuthill built the greatest concert hall in the world and 125 years later it is still one of the very best. In addition, Carnegie Hall was the one and only concert hall Tuthill ever built. How was this possible, with no knowledge, experience or even training? It is almost incomprehensible, but at the same time impossible to do this by luck, just as one could not build an airliner from all the parts by luck! He had an extraordinary instinct, and that is one of the most important things I look for in the people I employ. Even more surprising was that Carnegie Hall was built with three performance spaces, the largest and the smallest of which (Isaac Stern Auditorium/Ronald O. Perelman Stage and Weill Recital Hall) are the very best you will find anywhere, and a medium-sized one that became a cinema, as it did not work at all as a concert hall. In 2003, 112 years after first opening, it at last reopened as Zankel Hall, restoring the Hall's third performance space with an expanded volume blasted out of the bedrock. How could Tuthill have created two concert halls as good as anything in the world, and one that was useless?"

Gillinson asks a valid question, yet continual self-improvement and learning inevitably involves failures as well as successes. People unafraid to fail are often those who reach heights that could not otherwise be possible. Joel Klein has continually observed the correlation between great talent and ego. This may well be an innate human response, yet how much better for all concerned when not rife and eagerly displayed.

"Sit down and have a discussion with Clive and you see a mind engaged—not someone who's there to show off his own plumage, but to constantly learn and help out with challenges that the person across from him may be experiencing. Some people are so busy pontificating and you can tell they see themselves as an oracle. Clive has none of that."

Gillinson also knows his own limitations, gleaned from all those years as a practicing cellist, in a further testimony to the benefit of struggle, of occasional failures, of trying to understand the mechanics of self-improvement.

"Practicing the cello taught me a tremendous amount about discipline. As with almost everything I do, I was too obsessive, working hard rather than well a lot of the time. In retrospect, I should have practiced far better, more efficiently, concentrating on what I was trying to achieve with every bit of practice, rather than thinking it was the hours that counted. No one taught me how to practice *well.* One lesson I have learnt is that if things are bad or tough, it's still possible to learn from them, almost certainly even more than when all comes easily. The two things I do not have a lot of time for are regret and guilt, which always seem to be a waste of energy. If you don't want to do something, don't do it. Either change a bad decision or learn from it, but don't go ahead and then chastise yourself!"

Gillinson's view about fulfillment and happiness is that they are never achieved by chasing them for their own sake, but rather through engaging in activities that contribute to other people's lives.

"I spent my early years pursuing things that were about me—my motivation was essentially self-centered. There was so much I needed to prove to myself. When people now ask me for career advice, I always ask what they love doing and suggest they throw themselves 100% into it; opportunities will open up. I'm a clear example of that. I would never have gone into management but for a purely coincidental set of circumstances. The things I loved—maths, music and carpentry—all played a large part in revealing windows of opportunity. As a cellist I knew I would never become one of the greats, partly because my nerves as a performer made it hard for me to consistently give of my best. One of the surprising discoveries I made when becoming a manager was that those same nerves became a positive force in my ability to do the job; I found those pressures stimulating rather than undermining. Learning to know and understand ourselves is immensely valuable as well as very hard. All of us tend to avoid inconvenient facts if we have set our mind on doing something, frequently rejecting evidence that is 'hidden in plain sight'."

Humility

People of extraordinary and lasting accomplishment with nothing to prove almost always possess deep-rooted humility. What is it about the prevalent tendency toward one-upmanship? Why is it that pride is not always limited to the more interior pursuits of quiet knowledge, of meaningful achievement, of security borne of discipline and hard work? Must everything be on display? Credit-card companies, for example, began peddling Gold cards in the 1980s as a way to distinguish the truly elite from the merely creditworthy. The 1990s brought Platinum cards. The 2000s even saw Titanium cards. Will the 2010s offer a Palladium card? Can a Rhodium card be far behind? Perhaps just once the mailbox will carry a solicitation for an Aluminum card; humility and gratitude are ideal foils to materialism for its own sake.

Gillinson and his team always seek to foster humility in the young people with whom they engage, recognizing that it is among the most important underpinning values for life, while also encouraging achievement, individuality and self-worth—never as a commitment to self but to music, and through music to the lives of others.

"People often ask me about the most important characteristics of a great artist, and my response is always to start with humility. If artists don't want to go on learning and exploring until the last day of their life, they'll never be great. I have known some artists with exceptional talents, who lose their humility and end up giving good but unimportant performances: the greatest waste of all. Leonard Bernstein, for one, never stopped learning. A decision that typified this was toward the end of his life, when he threw away all of his Tchaikovsky symphony scores and bought new ones so that he could learn the music all over again, eliminating as far as possible his preconceptions. Or Slava Rostropovich—if you went to his room after a concert and started to eulogize about his performance, he wasn't interested in praise because all he was thinking about was tomorrow, and how that performance could be better. When somebody asked him if he had a favorite piece of music, he replied, 'The piece I'm playing now or I shouldn't be playing it.' It's how we push ourselves, demanding everything of every minute of our lives. That humility is so fundamental through every area of life. If you think you've arrived, it's all over."

Anne-Sophie Mutter also turns to Rostropovich as someone who fundamentally helped to shape her thinking:

"I was lucky enough to take part in string-trio performances with Slava and Bruno Giuranna. Back then, in the early '80s I had no experience whatsoever in playing chamber music. When we went through the Beethoven string trios, I remember one moment when Slava was almost screaming at me, saying, 'Why are you playing so loud there? There's nothing really interesting in that part, so just be quiet and listen to me!' I'll never forget that, because I was playing every note with pompous expressivity and thinking each was the last word and of the utmost importance. Learning to be a true part of any group is so crucial. And when it comes to accompanying someone else, Slava said—which I always convey to my students—that you almost have to project an out-of-body experience, because you have to give up your own persona in order to let another shine, to be able and willing to bring another person to the fore, serving the higher purpose that Slava was wonderful at putting into practice during rehearsals and concerts. The high intensity of his playing is a mantra for life, that each concert could possibly be the last one, that living on a precious and positive note shows every day as worthwhile. The present is a present and we have to live it like that. We all have to struggle, with dramatic and desperate moments for each of us, but we have only this one life, so let's get up and move forward."

Gillinson well remembers Rostropovich as an accompanist for his wife, the great soprano Galina Vishnevskaya:

"Slava was not only a truly remarkable cellist, but also a wonderful pianist, and in fact graduated from the Moscow Conservatory on the piano. When he accompanied Galina on the piano, he would spend the entire recital watching her and responding to what she was singing. Not only did he know all the music by heart, he hardly ever even looked down at the keyboard or his fingers—he was living every single piece of music that he played through her."

While humility may not seem as obviously needed with other professions as with an artist—a trial lawyer, for example, may possess an overblown ego, but within the courtroom his arrogance and skill, amidst well-defined law, can carry the day—it is altogether apparent that whether in the concert hall or around the dinner table, few people look forward to spending time with those who think that they have arrived, much less those who consider themselves the center of the world. Men and women have different talents, whether in front of a hundred orchestral musicians or before a trial jury, yet without humility there is no lifelong learning.

"There is no better example than Mariss Jansons," Gillinson observes.

"If, 40 years ago, you had asked people who the greatest conductors of the late 20th and early 21st centuries would be, his name would likely not have been on the list; he was relatively unknown at that time and never sought a media profile, and still does not. His focus is totally on serving the music and not himself. Today he's generally acknowledged to be one of the very greatest, and a central reason for this is that he's never stopped learning and wanting to learn, showing incredible humility in front of the music. Without that, all the rest becomes irrelevant. I remember Sir Colin Davis wistfully discussing one of his colleagues, undoubtedly one of the greatest conducting talents, who through lack of humility had become self-satisfied. His performances frequently ended up being showcases for himself rather than the music. Sir Colin's comment was: 'I am so glad that I was born with so much less talent than him, so that I have had to go on working and improving throughout my entire life.'"

In Polisi's over-40-year career, he has dealt with artists and teachers all the time; the very best of them are not at all arrogant, but constantly trying to get better.

"Clive's artistic integrity is at the highest level and excellence drives him, which is such a pleasure. We're so surrounded by mediocrity, which I've always said is like carbon monoxide: We can't smell or see it, but are just dead one day. It's only the mediocre types who are difficult to work with."

Jonathan Vaughan is instinctively drawn to people unafraid to question themselves and their teams, while always looking for ways of doing things better.

"A book that Clive recommended to me was Daniel Kahneman's brilliant and thought-provoking *Thinking, Fast and Slow*. He illustrates a point that Clive has talked about for years—we all have an ability to intuitively fill in the gaps in our knowledge without taking the trouble to check our assumptions. Managers and politicians all have the capacity to say of a situation about which they have little knowledge, 'Oh, I recognise this, it's just like....' In fact if they take the trouble to ask the right questions about the gaps in their knowledge, they might well find the situation and its solutions are quite different from those they initially understood."

With rare exceptions, Mutter finds musicians, like athletes, to be very focused on one particular subject in life and not very well rounded. She finds this irritating because, in order to contribute to society, people have to feel and know the world around them, to understand what is happening politically, to take part in many other subjects, to support more broad-minded school education, so that upcoming generations rely less on YouTube and more on reading.

> "Brahms used to say that every hour spent reading instead of practicing is a gain for our development as human beings. It's up to us as parents, in the few hours that we have left in a working week, to dedicate ourselves—particularly in the first 10 years—to offering our children as much choice in pastimes and hobbies as possible, to stimulate the neurons in their brains, to connect and reconnect and re-reconnect, because this is what's going to help them to be more critical and sensitized to everything in life. These early years are so crucial, because that's when the seeds are planted for the interests they later develop, not only being a consumer, but actively taking part in the process of building something or reading or just dreaming by themselves. This has nothing to do with wonderful and useful tools like the iPad, but they shouldn't be so prominent in a small child's life. This mindset also keeps people young throughout life. Alzheimer's is essentially nonexistent among professional musicians. The brains can be ageless… if only the knees wouldn't give in!"

Doing benefit work, building an orphanage, volunteering time, touching others, being a parent, making a positive difference in others' lives: These and innumerable other pursuits beyond oneself is where life comes together and is the most meaningful.

Mutter makes a telling observation:

> "Schiller used to say that it's about brotherhood and sisterhood, and we're more similar to one another than most of us would like to acknowledge. That's partly why music exists—to bring us together, to have us experience the same emotions regardless of our cultural roots or religious backgrounds, which may be totally different. But we can in fact feel the same!"

25

Loyalty & Behaving Well

Gillinson has always placed a high priority on loyalty. He consistently conveys to his staff that it does not matter how badly a customer or anyone else acts; the response always has to be to behave well and professionally, never responding in kind.

> "To me, the foundation on which all value systems need to be built, and the fundamental cornerstone of morality, is to treat others as you would have them treat you. It also eliminates being defined by competitors or enemies. We all fail and eventually erode our own values if we allow ourselves to respond badly to bad behavior, which, like everyone else, I've done at times and hope I've learned to handle tough situations better over the years. I used to find it very hard not to respond to unpleasantness or force in kind, but behaving well can be far more meaningful and powerful."

Loyalty flows naturally from this mindset. One of the people who deeply embedded the importance of loyalty in Gillinson was Rostropovich, who always supported his friends no matter how challenging the circumstances or bad the consequences.

> "Slava once told me that he had decided it was time to reduce his workload, as he was getting too tired. He thought the answer was to double his fee so that he could take more time off, whilst still maintaining his earnings. When I saw him some time later, I asked whether it had worked and he said, 'No, Clive, it's a disaster! Everybody is paying the new fee, so I'm working just as hard as before!' The amazing thing about him was that, based on his belief in friendship, he never set a fee for the LSO. He would simply say to me, 'Clive, my fee is what you tell me the LSO can afford.'"

Literature also taught Gillinson the inherent value of behaving well, which has had a lasting influence on his beliefs and values. Biographies of Gandhi and Mandela became two clear focal points. Those whom he has most admired do not fight evil with evil or force with force, but always look for ways to achieve what they believe in by engaging people with powerful ideas and fundamental values.

Given how difficult Gillinson's initial time as manager of the LSO became, behaving well was clearly counter to instinct, yet ultimately the only effective way to achieve meaningful change. He recognized that almost from the start, knowing that he had to absorb anger rather than return it. Occasionally he would respond in kind, but came to understand that this was invariably a mistake, albeit a tough one from which to learn. Absorbing anger requires inner strength and offers the opportunity of taking people somewhere else, whereas fighting it in kind almost always leads to everyone getting entrenched.

Having a family to go back to, a spouse and children—a source of unquestioned love and care— can be crucial, and that was true for Gillinson:

> "It was incredibly important to have a place where I could unload and share some of it, whilst also getting emotional support. In addition to my family, I was fortunate that there were a number of players in the LSO who understood the nature and challenges of the job, as well as the need for change; this was a relatively small group at first, but over time it began to grow. At my early orchestra meetings I was largely on my own—a tough and very unpleasant learning curve. I was also very lucky in the chairmen of the orchestra with whom I worked, and three of them—Lennox McKenzie, John Lawley and Jonathan Vaughan—served as great partners for most of my 21 years as managing director."

In the end, responding in kind to aggressive behavior becomes a war of attrition and no one wins, least of all the organization itself. Fighting fire with fire leaves everyone burnt. Yet if it goes against instinct, how can people take a step back and will themselves to behave well, retaining objectivity and calm? Gillinson has seen that everyone needs at least one person on whom they can rely, who has the courage to be totally honest and is willing to be a sounding board for exploring challenging situations or problems, whether a relative, friend or career coach.

> "It is about learning how to manage tough situations and people, and taking complete responsibility for your own behavior. People

who fight aggression in kind are unlikely to change, mainly because they usually don't want to. The chances of them seeking or listening to advice regarding their behavior are small. I don't want this sort of person working for me, nor do I want to work with them as outside partners. The other challenge with people who aggressively respond to difficult situations is that it can take a lot of courage to play their behavior back to them, as there is a good chance that they will shoot the messenger!"

Gillinson consistently reinforces the message about loyalty and behaving well with his staff:

"When having to deal with very demanding situations, as in a business negotiation in which we were once involved, I would thank our team after every meeting for the superb way they handled themselves. They never met anger with anger and we all stayed cool under challenging and provocative circumstances. Towards the end of the negotiation, the other party had still not achieved their key objective; their leader leaned across the table and almost spat out the words: 'Tomorrow you'll come crawling to us on your hands and knees, begging to accept what we're offering you today, and it will no longer be available.' We quietly reiterated that we were not prepared to go down that route. The following day, having tested us to their limit, we were able to arrive at a mutually acceptable solution. One of the most important outcomes of that negotiation was that we ended up with a better relationship than before. Saving and maintaining relationships in such testing situations is vital, and far less likely if you try to fight fire with fire."

Why is this philosophy of behaving well—cool and rational—so foreign to so many people given its obvious benefits, let alone case study after case study?

"Through my early days at the LSO, I started to learn that even if we couldn't find a solution today, we would ultimately find one. There is simply no substitute for learning from experience. Negotiations can involve parties shouting and screaming at each other across a table, with everybody throwing hand grenades. Where does that get you? That can damage relationships so much that, even if it is ultimately possible to save them, endless hours are required to do so, time that could have been used far more constructively. I learned this lesson the hard way. Early on in my management career, there was a particular manager with whom we had to work on many aspects of our business, and we had all become utterly frustrated as he always put the orchestra at the bottom of his priority list; he was too wrapped up with nurturing his own profile. He did not understand that if we did well, he would also look good. In the end, out of pure frustration, I exploded and told him exactly what I thought of his behavior. It took at least three months before he could even look me in the eye again, and far longer before we were able to re-establish a meaningful working relationship: a colossal waste of time and effort just for the satisfaction of one explosion! I swore to myself never to repeat that. I still ended up doing it again a few years later, with a different person and similar results. Lesson *really* learned!"

The positive aspect of this decision was demonstrated to Gillinson at Carnegie Hall, when he had to issue a warning to a staff member for aggressive and intimidating behavior toward a colleague:

"When I raised this with him, he said that a previous executive and artistic director had behaved in a similar way towards him. I was able to make it clear that neither I nor any of our senior team would ever behave like that with any staff member, and that I considered such behavior totally unacceptable. He had no room left to argue the point and his behavior changed. Clearly, in order to develop a positive company culture, this has to come from the top. Little can be achieved by diktat without leading by example."

Respect Across the Board

Gillinson recalls a night in Japan that summed up for him Rostropovich's ability to communicate with anybody and everybody, a central lesson with continuing impact:

"The emperor and empress of Japan attended an LSO gala concert at Suntory Hall that Slava was conducting. At the end of the concert I took him to the Imperial Greeting Room at the Hall where he and the emperor and empress, great music lovers themselves, had a very friendly and warm conversation, after which they departed.

We all went out for dinner and got back to the hotel at about 1 a.m. Slava then said, 'Clive, tomorrow we go to the Tsukiji (the famous fish market). We meet downstairs at 5 a.m.' The Tsukiji is incredibly dramatic; they auction off huge numbers of tuna literally in minutes. The atmosphere is electric and bears no relationship to any other aspect of life I have ever seen in Japan, with everyone shouting and gesticulating in a totally un-Japanese way. Slava had clearly been there many times before and loved it, and was mimicking all the auctioneers and buyers. When the auction was finished he said, 'Now we go to see my friend.' His friend owned one of the tuna stalls and, when we arrived, which by then was about 6:30 a.m., he gave us what he called the best part of the tuna… and sake. Partway through the conversation, Slava asked him how his daughter was. 'She's studying in Paris at the Sorbonne.' Slava immediately grabbed the phone and called her in Paris. I don't know anyone else who could have traveled the journey from the emperor and empress to the fish market within a few hours, and been completely at home and loved in both."

Rostropovich had the most remarkable gift for friendship—central to every aspect of his life—that Gillinson has ever experienced:

"He once explained to me why it mattered so much to him. He and his wife Galina took the great Russian novelist, Alexander Solzhenitsyn, into their home after he lost everything and had nowhere to live because of his writings about the Gulag political prisons. Almost immediately, all of Slava's concerts and travel rights were cancelled, and this was the start of the most terrible time of his life. Overnight most of the people he had thought were his friends seemed to be avoiding him, and when he walked down the street, erstwhile friends would somehow be walking on the other side and not notice him. He said it was during this time that he understood who his real friends were. He valued beyond words those who were brave enough to maintain their friendship with him, despite the risk to themselves."

Loyalty and integrity are tightly interwoven:

"During this traumatic period, Rostropovich was offered a recital in Siberia, in an aircraft hangar for several thousand people. He and his pianist traveled to the venue, but when they arrived there was no audience; whoever was in charge had forgotten to publicise the concert. He asked if there was literally no one there to hear the concert, and was told that there were five ex-political prisoners who had somehow heard about it and traveled across the snow to hear him play, but that of course he should not play just for five people. He insisted on performing his full recital program, as well as encores, all to a standing ovation by the five. A defining aspect of Slava as both an artist and a human being was the fact that he treated this performance with the same love and respect as a Carnegie Hall concert. Boulez was another remarkable person in so many ways. One of his most endearing traits showed itself on every LSO tour; he was the only conductor who would take the road and personnel managers and the librarian out for dinner, to thank them for their largely invisible work."

In considering Gillinson's contributions, Mackenzie points to the history-proven truism that leaders are enthusiastically followed because people trust and respect them, not because of their position per se.

"Clive is very good at relationships with people from all walks of life. He is also an incredibly hard worker, forever first in the office. He knows the value of having and keeping good and talented people on his team. One of his final tasks at the LSO was to persuade me to return to the fold as chairman after a long break. I was reluctant, as it's an exhausting task alongside my violin-playing responsibilities. But he was persuasive. A new managing director had to be found and he wanted me on the panel in charge of the offer. Happily we found that person in Kathryn McDowell, who remains as managing director to this day, and I remained chairman for 11 years after my conversation with Clive! The knighthood he received was richly deserved and an extremely popular award."

Vaughan saw firsthand how Gillinson values loyalty:

"Clive has always cultivated a sense amongst the workforce that they should look after their partners and collaborators, almost more so if they fall on hard times. He instils a strong ethical and moral code in which you never walk away from a supporter or partner if they can no longer help you, with a responsibility to help them long past their usefulness to your organisation."

Natural Empathy

Corporate and nonprofit history is littered with examples of executives who may have started out their jobs with idealism and discipline, yet became ever more unbearable as their responsibilities, salaries and stock options increased. This hardly needs to be a quid pro quo. For every such manager, there are those on the other side whose egos do not require skyscraper attention and who take corporate social responsibility seriously. Why do some descend into the former camp, while others thrive within the latter? Taking a step back from the moments and tasks at hand, those able to recognize what matters in life—regardless of position—have consistently shown themselves to be happier and more content than those who are constantly driven by their ego.

Why does the ego so often cross that line? S. Mark Young, a professor at the University of Southern California's Marshall School of Business, points out that narcissists may do the most damage at the top, but they can disrupt workplaces at all levels:

> "They possess very little empathy and have grandiose views of themselves, leading to feelings of entitlement and a constant need for admiration. Narcissists are cutthroat and scheming; they tend to dominate the conversation and will do just about anything to be the center of attention, even if it's negative attention."

Yet despite our current age of self-aggrandizement, a genuine belief in behaving well is not necessarily counter-cultural. Empathy, curiosity and creativity are natural human gifts, be they expressed through the stage, visual arts, technology, sports, language, math, nature, humor, relationships, leadership.... Discovering and then actively using these gifts cannot help but advance us as individuals, families, organizations and society—continually fostering bottom-line results and top-line experiences.

More and more people across our planet are standing up for the greater good, eager to embrace Nelson Mandela's fought-for observation:

"It is better to lead from behind and to put others in front, especially when you celebrate victory when nice things occur. You take the front line when there is danger. Then people will appreciate your leadership."

Postscript

In one of those intriguing coincidences that life continually offers, Clive and I—avid lifelong readers—have considered Dostoevsky's *Crime and Punishment* our favorite novel since opening its singular pages. It also became my catalyst to learn Russian beginning in high school, given an intense desire to read and savor it in the original language. I adapted the current book's title, *Better to Speak of It*, from the fourth chapter, when Raskolnikov ponders what he considers the cunning of his mother and sister in keeping from him details about the latter's marriage: better not to speak of it. Removing that single word "not" frees up a landscape of transparency, openness and curiosity that courses through each of the lived-through and learned-from experiences within the present chapters.

Robert Rimm
June 2016

Credits

Images:

Gillinson at desk © Libby Rice
Ian Martin courtesy of Ian Martin
Michael Tilson Thomas courtesy of Michael Tilson Thomas
Joel Klein © The Aspen Institute/photo by Clint Spaulding
Joseph Polisi © Christian Steiner
Jonathan Vaughan courtesy of Jonathan Vaughan
Anthony Marx © Jason Torres
Gillinson with Sanford Weill © Don Perdue
Jessye Norman © Universal Music Group
Emanuel Ax © Lisa Marie Mazzucco
Glenn Lowry © Peter Ross
Joyce DiDonato © Simon Pauly
Paul King courtesy of Paul King
Allison Vulgamore © J.D. Scott
Lennox Mackenzie © Wendy Spon
Rostropovich & Gillinson © Mike Powell/ *The Times* (London)
Queen Elizabeth The Queen Mother, Rostropovich & Gillinson © Suzie Maeder
Slava gorilla © Diana Salthouse
Matías Tarnopolsky © Kat Wade
Anne-Sophie Mutter © Monika Höfler
Dvora Lewis courtesy of Dvora Lewis
Joseph Nye by Chatham House. "Joseph Nye" by Chatham House
    is licensed under CC BY 2.0.

Cover:

Original painting by Jessica Libor
Gillinson © Chris Lee

CPSIA information can be obtained
at www.ICGtesting.com
Printed in the USA
BVOW08s1647150117

473308BV00006B/2/P